EMPLOYEE HANDBOOK
Australia

ROBERTA CAVA

Employee Handbook

Australia

Roberta Cava

Published by Cava Consulting

cavaconsulting@ozemail.com.au

Discover other titles by Roberta Cava at
www.dealingwithdifficultpeople.info

National Library of Australia

Cataloguing-in-publication data:

ISBN 9780992448929

BOOKS BY ROBERTA CAVA

All can be purchased from Amazon Books

Non-Fiction

Dealing with Difficult People
(International best-seller since 1990 with 24 publishers – in 18 languages in over 100 countries)
Kein Problem mit Schwierigen Menschen (German)
Tratando con Gente Difícil (Spanish)
Traiter avec des personnes difficiles (French)
Comunicareaea cu oameni dificili (Romanian)
Dealing with Difficult Situations – at Work and at Home
Tratando con Situationes Dificiles (Spanish)
Dealing with Difficult Spouses and Children
Tratando con Cónyuges y Niños Difíciles
Dealing with Difficult Relatives and In-Laws
Tratando con parientes difíciles y en leyes
Dealing with School Bullying
Tratando con la Intimidación en la Escouela (Spanish)
Dealing with Workplace Bullying
Tratando con Intimidación en el lugar de trabajo
Keeping Our Children Safe
Mantenera Nuestros Hijos Seguros (Spanish)
Dealing with Domestic Violence and Child Abuse
Retirement Village Bullies
Just say no
What am I going to do with the rest of my life?
Interpersonal Communication at Work
Change? Not me!
Creative Problem-Solving & Decision-Making
Customer Service that Works
Teambuilding
How Women can advance in business
Before Tying the Knot – Questions couples must ask each other before they marry!
Survival Skills for Supervisors and Managers
Human Resources at its Best!
Human Resources Policies and Procedures - Australia
Employee Handbook
Easy Come – Hard to go – The Art of Hiring, Disciplining and Firing Employees
Time and Stress – Today's silent killers

Take Command of your Future – Make things Happen!
The Presenter
Belly Laughs for All! – Volumes 1 to 8
Australian Trivia
Trivia and More
Wisdom of the World! The happy, sad & wise things in life!
Covid-19 200 Days – Facts and Fun
Covid-19 200-400 Days – Facts and Fun
Covid 400-600 Days – Facts and Fun

Fiction

I can do it! The sky's the limit!
Twists and Turns
Treacherous Livelihoods
Life Gets Complicated
Life Goes On
Life Gets Better
That Something Special
Something Missing

EMPLOYEE HANDBOOK
AUSTRALIA

Table of Contents

Introduction

Your company Employee Handbook should cover all the rules and regulations that an employee is expected to know and follow. They are an employee's guide that explains a company's rules and regulations.

On the first day of the person's employment, s/he is given a copy of the company Employee Handbook and after a week is asked to sign an agreement stating that s/he has read the handbook and understands its content. This way both employees and employers are protected.

- The employee will be protected because s/he will know the company rules and regulations.
- The employer will be protected because if the employee breaks any of the company rules and regulations s/he won't be able to claim innocence if s/he has confirmed that s/he knew and understood them.

Employee Handbooks normally back up a company's formal Human Resources Policy and Procedures Manual, so if your company doesn't have one, it should consider preparing one. Cava Consulting has made this easier and companies can order one by going to: www.cavaconsulting.com/orderbooks.html.

Employment laws are constantly changing. As a result, this handbook is accurate to the best of the knowledge and belief of the author. The examples given are those used in Australia, therefore it's important that you check your own Federal and State laws to adapt these regulations to meet the demands of your area.

This Handbook, does, however, provide you and your company with a good deal of common-sense management. Armed with that advice, companies will be better prepared to undertake the everyday performance of their Human Resources Departments.

It's essential that all Human Resources Practitioners check:

- their Enterprise and Union Agreements; and
- their State and Federal Laws, Employee Relations and Labour Laws.

The items listed are guidelines only and some just give background information, so you know what to put in your company's employee handbook. Some of the items may not apply to your kind of industry. Those that do can be adapted to suit your company's way of doing things.

The Handbook is not designed to replace professional advice and is intended as a learning tool only. It's important to note that Cava Consulting makes no warranty of any kind, expressed or implied, with regard to the content of this handbook. We recommend that, as required, you seek further advice on the use of any document or information, particularly where you are unsure of any aspect of implementation.

Where you see the word (Company) you would insert your company name.

Chapter 1

Corporate History

(This is where you would explain the company history, where your offices are situated, the company's major departments and possibly list their executive staff names.)

Orientation

ID Card, Badges and Security Passes

To increase professionalism and security, employees will be issued with photo ID cards. These cards will be used to access most areas of the building. Sensitive areas of the workplace may require higher security measures. Employees will need to produce their ID cards for all restricted areas and should carry them at all times. Failure to display this ID card may be interpreted as a form of misconduct.

Name badges will be issued to all staff and are to be worn while on duty, either on or off the premises. Name badges are a form of employee and company recognition. At (Company) we have found a positive reaction from clients to the provision of nametags.

ID cards and name badges will be replaced at no charge to the staff member. Lost or stolen cards are to be reported immediately to the Human Resources Department. If you repeatedly lose or misplace your ID card or name badge, you may be asked to pay for production costs.

Security Passes will be used in the lifts and may allow staff to have access only to their own floor of the building.

Health Insurance

(Company) has made provision for employees to participate in a company health insurance scheme at reduced fees. Even though employees are well covered for accidents and illness on the job, we believe it is good practice to have health insurance for employees and their families. Health insurance offers better care, more flexibility in choice of doctor, hospital and type of treatment.

The joining of the company health insurance scheme is not compulsory but is offered as a benefit to employees.

Life, Disability and Salary Continuance Insurance

(Company) offers employees the opportunity to join an insurance fund at a reduced price. This option is available to staff who have been working for (Company) for a six-month period. The company fund has been established to enable employees the maximum benefit possible at the most economical price. Contact our Human Resources Department to learn more about this company benefit.

Special Requirements

Medical Examinations

Medical examinations may be required before an appointment is made for some positions. Where the position requires such an examination, this is to be stated at the employment interview.

Medical examinations may be either pre-employment or pre-placement. Employers have sought medical advice on the physical and sometimes mental abilities of applicants for job functions, their workers compensation risks and eligibility for superannuation schemes.

If a medical examination is used as part of a selection decision, an employer needs to be specific in terms of why it is being used and what it is looking for.

Orientation of New Employee

On the employee's first day of work the Human Resources Officer will give assistance in completing the documentation and distribute the documents as required. The employee will take part in (Company's) Induction Program.

The Supervisor will go over the employee's position description with the new employee. They will discuss the employee's pay schedule, hours of work, lunch and coffee breaks, parking, security (including removal of company property) safety and emergency procedures. The Supervisor will give the employee a tour of the facilities and initiate whatever training is deemed necessary for the employee to become productive.

The Supervisor will appoint a long-term employee or friendly colleague who will "adopt" the new employee. This person will act as their guide. This colleague shows the new employee where the washroom is, when and where to go for coffee and lunch breaks and makes him/her feel welcome with other colleagues. New employees will be taught the internal phone and computer systems and other common internal procedures such as paper flow, shipping and receiving, scheduling and safety. This takes the edge off the situation for the new employee in a way that the Supervisor could not. It also introduces him/her to the new peer group. The Supervisor's role is to set the atmosphere, then back off to let it work.

The Supervisor will set up an appointment two weeks after employee's commencement with the company to discuss any problems and see how well the employee is fitting in with the company.

Code of conduct

(Company) has a Code of Conduct that sets ethical standards for (Company) employees.

The Code of Conduct contains the following principles. Employee:

- must comply with all laws in everything that they do;
- must behave honestly and with integrity at all times;
- personal dealings must be kept separate from their business dealings;

- must not use, or attempt to use, information obtained in the course of their employment with (Company) for any purpose other than for the proper purposes of (Company's) business;
- must not do anything that actually conflicts, or might possibly result in a conflict, with the duties and obligations that they have as an employee of (Company); and
- must not seek, or accept, improper benefits (for themselves or for any third parties) from those doing business or seeking to do business with (Company).

Confidentiality

Employees of (Company) will have access to confidential information, so must only use information obtained as an employee of (Company) in the proper performance of their duties as an employee of (Company).

In particular, they must not disclose information about customers, fellow employees or (Company's) business to anyone (including a fellow employee) who is not authorised to receive that information.

Always keep confidentiality in mind. Don't discuss work related matters in the building lifts. Don't read (Company) documents on public transport, as you never know who will be looking over your shoulder!

Company Property Declaration

During your employment with (Company) you will be supplied with company property that will assist you in carrying out your responsibilities.

You have a duty of care to ensure the items provided are looked after and are not intentionally damaged. On termination you will return all company property.

Chapter 2

Recruitment

(Company) as an Equal Employment Opportunity Employer, aims to ensure the best available employees are given the opportunity to be considered for each position. Accordingly, all employees and applicants for positions at (Company) must be treated:

- According to their:
    - skills, including both the task and people skills necessary for effective performance in a position;
    - qualifications;
    - abilities;
    - aptitudes; and

- Without regard to factors such as:
    - age;
    - race;
    - marital status;
    - gender;
    - disability;
    - pregnancy, or
    - sexual preference.

- (Company) will attract and retain high performing staff by:
    - offering attractive working conditions;
    - a commitment to professional development and training; and
    - the opportunity for employees to follow career paths. To achieve this, whenever possible (Company):

        i. encourages employees to manage their own careers;

ii.   is committed to redeploying and retraining existing employees; and

iii.   advertising all vacant positions internally before advertising externally.

(Company) is committed to making maximum effort to re-deploy and retain existing employees. Accordingly, personnel on redeployment will be given first consideration for vacancies for which they apply and are suitably qualified.

All positions within (Company) will be open to the internal network before any external recruitment effort is made. Information will be made available through employee email and posted on notice boards.

Existing Employees

All employees of (Company) are encouraged to apply for internally advertised positions. Applicant should advise his/her Supervisor of his/her intentions to apply for an internal position. It's up to the proposed Supervisor to speak to the employee's existing Supervisor to determine suitability. The proposed Supervisor will have access to the employee's personnel file that they will sign out and return to the Human Resources Department.

Staff will be considered for positions based on the length of time spent as an employee, previous performance reviews and other relevant factors, such as commendations or written warnings. Before being eligible to apply for a vacant position, employee is expected to have served a period of no less than 12 months in his/her present role for sustained performance to be realised/assessed.

Human Resources will supply interested candidates with the appropriate forms to apply.

Temporary appointments are made when an employee:

- goes on parental leave;

- switches to part time work; or
- because there is not enough staff to handle excessive workloads.

Temporary appointments (i.e.: to cover Parental Leave vacancies) are to be clearly stated on the Job Vacancy Circular and list the conditions of the appointment.

The replacement employee must be informed that the employee on leave or working part-time has the right to return to the position and that the appointment is temporary. Employees, who are temporarily appointed to positions at a higher grade, will not be eligible for a permanent upgrade, if they have mutually agreed to relieve in the position while another employee is on leave. However, higher duties allowance will apply if work is performed for a minimum of five consecutive workdays using 'Higher Duties Allowance' form.

Criminal History Check [Optional]

All persons selected for appointment to a role within (Company) must be requested to submit to a Police Records Check prior to their appointment being confirmed. This policy applies to all forms of external recruitment (full, part-time, casual or contract), whether sourced through an external agency or otherwise.

Before you commence work with (Company) you must apply to have a criminal history check undertaken by the police and the results of this check must be satisfactory to us.

Appointment to Lower Grade Roles

There are four ways that an employee's appointment to a lower graded role can occur. All must have written documentation showing that the employee has approved of the change:

- an employee applies for a lower graded job;

- an employee accepts a lower graded role due to a restructure;
- an employee accepts redeployment to a lower graded role as an alternative to retrenchment; or
- an employee requests a transfer and the only suitable position is a lower graded job.

Work Experience Students

Work Experience is a program instigated by the (State) Education Department to give secondary students over the age of 15 (usually in Years 10, 11 or 12) the opportunity to spend one week in a workplace environment to further develop their relevant employment-related skills.

Corporations are asked to offer these students a chance to 'watch and learn' on the job whilst being fully covered for Workers Compensation and Insurance by the Education Department. The organisation is asked to contribute up to $10 per day to cover the students' out-of-pocket expenses incurred through travel and lunches during the week. Maximum payment is $50 for the week.

It is important for Supervisors to ensure students offered placement in (Company) can utilise their current skills to increase their particular competencies in their chosen field.

New Employee Required Documents

Curriculum Vitae / Resume

A current Curriculum Vitae / Resume must be provided by all persons applying for roles within (Company). This policy applies to all forms of employment (full, part-time, casual or contract) whether sourced through an external recruitment firm or otherwise. External recruitment firms must provide this information at the time of initial recruitment into (Company).

A minimum of one document within each of the following categories is required as a minimum standard in establishing the following key criteria relevant to recruitment within (Company):

Identity/Citizenship

- birth certificate;
- passport; or
- driver's license.
- address
- property tax notice;
- rental agreement;
- utilities account; or
- bank statement.

Signed documents of the following types are required to substantiate the claims of educational or work history:

Education

- degree;
- diploma;
- university or education transcript;
- trades certificate; or
- secondary college/school record of achievement.

Prior Employment

- group certificate (covering period of prior employment);
- employment separation certificate (issued by prior employer);
- names of former supervisors and how to reach them; and
- certificates of achievement.

Note: Original documents must be sighted, and copies made for placement into the new employee's personnel file that will be retained in the Human Resources Department.

Personnel File Records:

Employees are entitled to have access to their records as well as those of employees who report directly to them and may make notes and photocopy information from the record. Photocopies should be permitted on request without cost to the individual. Employees should provide appropriate proof of identity before access is granted.

Subject to the approval of the employee's immediate supervisor, personnel files will also be available to other supervisors when the employee is being considered for a position in that department.

Employees may nominate a representative to access their record on their behalf. In such cases, access should only be granted with the written consent of the employee. Access should be given at a mutually convenient time and be supervised to ensure that information is not removed from the file.

Personnel files may be reviewed during normal office hours. An employee wishing to view his or her personnel file is asked to first call Human Resources to ensure an employee will be available to obtain the file.

Personnel files will be reviewed in the offices of the Human Resources Department. Under special circumstances, personnel files may be temporarily removed with the approval of the Human Resources Manager.

Adverse Notations:

Where any adverse notation or disciplinary action is recorded on a personal file, the person concerned must be shown the notation and permitted to add written comments. The person should be invited to sign the notation, but should s/he decline to do so, no further action is to be taken in this regard other than to record the invitation and the refusal. Companies should establish independent review committees to review all files –

especially those that have disputed adverse notations and amendments to files.

Use of Staff Records:

Generally, staff records may only be used within a company for purposes specified at the time the information is collected and by officers with the authority to access these records. The informed consent of the record subject should be obtained before any other use of a staff record is made. Besides the employee, only authorised employees should have access to these records (such as Human Resources, Payroll staff and Supervisors of the employee).

Privacy Guidelines

All companies are obliged to comply with privacy legislation. The Privacy (Private Sector) Amendment Act of 21st December 2001 is based on ten National Privacy Principles (NPPs) dealing with the following areas:

1. collection of personal information;
2. use and disclosure of personal information;
3. data quality;
4. data security;
5. openness;
6. access to and correction of personal information;
7. identifiers of individuals;
8. anonymity;
9. trans-border data flows; and
10. sensitive information.

Chapter 3

Leave

The primary purpose of annual leave is to provide employees with a meaningful break from work for rest and rejuvenation.

Entitlement

Full time and part time employees will be entitled to 4 weeks' paid annual leave upon each completed year of service.

Payment for annual leave for part time employees will be calculated on a pro-rata basis of the average actual hours worked in the previous 12 months and will be paid at the hourly rate applicable at the time of taking the leave.

Annual leave should be taken within 12 months of it falling due, except where management has agreed to allow a further accrual for a special reason such as an extended holiday. An employee will give a minimum of 3 weeks' notice when requesting approval for annual leave. (Company) may direct an employee to take annual leave that has accrued by giving the employee 2 month's notice. In either case, a shorter notice period may be permitted by mutual agreement.

Conditions

1. Annual leave schedules shall be determined by (Company) and must necessarily be dependent upon the operating conditions. Effort will be made to schedule vacations during a period convenient to the employee.
2. Employees are expected to take their annual leave when earned and will not be permitted to draw annual leave pay in lieu of time off.
3. Employees will be permitted to carry over up to two weeks' of their earned annual leave into the following year. This annual leave must be taken within the first quarter of the next calendar year or it will be forfeited.

The carry-over annual leave entitlement must be approved by their Department Head.

4. If a recognised Statutory Holiday falls within the scheduled annual leave, employee will be entitled to an additional day off in lieu of the Statutory Holiday.

5. Employees may split their annual leave into more than one period, but not more than three if approved by their Department Head.

6. Annual leave pay will be computed by multiplying the established basic average scheduled work week, times the straight-time hourly rate in effect for the position normally held by employee at the start of his/her annual leave.

7. If employee's service is terminated, they shall be paid at current rates for annual leave earned, but not taken.

8. An employee who was sick during his/her annual leave, may reschedule this time with the approval of their Department Head and provided a Doctor's certificate is produced.

Minimum Period of Annual Leave to be taken each year

It is an essential requirement that during the year all employees:

- take all of their annual leave entitlement; and
- are absent for a minimum of ten consecutive business days during that period of leave.

Public Holidays

Any period of annual leave is exclusive of any public holidays falling within that period.

Annual Leave Loading (Optional)

Leave loading will be paid to eligible employees at the time of their anniversary of service date.

Leave loading will be 17.5% of ordinary time earnings subject to a maximum payment. For the year 20___, the maximum payment will be equal to 17.5% of the equivalent of 4 weeks' salary of an employee on an annual salary of $_____.

In each subsequent year, the maximum payment will be increased effective 1 January by the annual percentage change in average weekly earnings: full time adult ordinary time earnings (all persons, all industries) in August.

Shift workers who work a 5-day 8- hour rotating shift roster will be paid a leave loading of 19.2%.

Payment for the period of leave

If annual leave is requested and approved at least three weeks before the date of commencement of leave, the employee will be paid full pay for all pays due during the period of leave. Alternatively, they can request that the pays continue to be transferred to their nominated bank account each fortnight.

Long Service Leave

Long Service Leave is paid leave granted to employees with a required minimum amount of continuous service in recognition of their ongoing contribution to the organisation.

The qualifying period of service and the conditions relating to the entitlements to Long Service Leave are governed by the current (Company) Enterprise Agreement and relevant State and Federal legislation.

Basic Entitlement

It may be necessary to refer to the specific terms and conditions of employment of certain employees to ascertain long service leave benefits.

Each employee will be entitled to 13 weeks long service leave, or an amount of leave as calculated under this policy, at actual rates of pay on the completion of 15 years' continuous service with (Company), and thereafter an additional 4 1/3 weeks' leave on completion of each subsequent 5 years of service.

An employee who has completed at least 10 years' service may access all or part of their accrued long service leave, provided that the amount of leave taken is at least 4 weeks. Such leave to be taken at a time agreed between the employee and Supervisor.

Payment in lieu of leave on termination

When an employee terminates employment or the employment is terminated by (Company) for any cause other than serious misconduct and the employee has completed 10 years or more continuous employment, the employee will be entitled to payment in lieu of long service leave less any long service leave already taken by the employee.

Time of Taking Leave

Leave must be granted and taken as soon as practicable after becoming due and have regard to the needs of the workplace but may be postponed or taken in 2 or more periods by agreement between the employee and Supervisor.

Granting Leave in Advance

(Company) may, by agreement with an employee, allow long service leave before an employee's right to long service leave has accrued. When such leave is taken in advance, the employee will not become entitled to further leave or to payment in lieu of the period for which leave was taken before its accrued date.

Payment of Salary during Leave

Salary for the period of leave may, at (Company)'s option, be paid in full at the commencement of long service leave or at the time it would have been paid had the employee remained on duty. If the latter option is utilised, the salary will be paid into the nominated account into which the employee's normal fortnightly salary is paid.

If an employee dies prior to or during a period of long service leave, (Company) will pay the amount calculated, using the employee's actual rate of pay at the time of his/her death, for the period of leave untaken or not yet paid to the employee's legal representative.

Actual rates of pay mean the actual salary of the employee for a normal weekly number of hours of work immediately prior to the time of taking each period of long service leave.

Such salary will not include:

- shift premiums;
- overtime;
- penalty rates;
- commissions;
- bonuses; or
- allowances

payable to the employee when working.

Holidays and Annual Leave

Any period of long service leave will be inclusive of any public holiday falling within that time but will be exclusive of any period of annual leave.

Employment during Long Service Leave

Employees must not engage in any paid employment whilst they are on long service leave without specific authorisation of (Company). Any employee who engages in such employment will forfeit the right to payment for long service leave for the period in which they are engaged in such employment. If the employee has been paid in advance for leave, s/he will repay to (Company) that amount.

Public Holidays and Picnic Days

Public holidays are days declared as such by Federal or State Governments, usually through a Government Gazette. There are 10 standard public holidays in Australia:

- New Year's Day;
- Australia Day;

- Good Friday;
- Easter Saturday;
- Easter Monday;
- ANZAC Day;
- Queen's Birthday;
- Eight-Hour/Labour Day;
- Christmas Day; and
- Boxing Day (replaced by Proclamation Day in SA).

Other special holidays for particular sections of the workforce may also be granted, such as Bank Holiday, show day, union picnic days or special award holidays.

The typical clause in an award or agreement on public/special holidays usually contains the following elements:

- a list of the prescribed holidays for that award or agreement;
- provision when a holiday falls on a Saturday or Sunday (usually, but not always, nominating an alternative day);
- other provisions for substitution of holiday if the employee is required to work on the original day;
- payment for working on a holiday;
- provision for minimum payment and crib time for working on a holiday; and
- special provision relating to shift workers.

As a general rule, the entitlement to a public holiday is not removed because an employee is on leave. However, there are different rules for the various types of leave:

Annual Holiday: Where a holiday falls while an employee is taking annual leave; the employee is entitled to that holiday with pay.

Special Leave

Sick Leave: An employee on sick leave continues to be employed and is, therefore entitled to the public holiday with pay, even if the person's sick leave entitlement has been exhausted. Sick leave will be given:

a) Where an employee is disabled due to sickness or injury and is unable to perform his/her duties, benefits will be payable for entitled sick days.

b) The employee's Department Manager must be notified on the first day of the employee's illness or injury and must be kept informed if the sick leave continues.

c) Unused portions of benefit level entitlements in a year cannot be carried forward into the next year.

d) Where a sickness or injury extends beyond a period of three consecutive days, a certificate or statement of the attending doctor or physician may be required upon return to active employment.

e) The company may require an employee be examined by a doctor acceptable to the company when prolonged or frequent absences from work occur or when an employee is unable to satisfactorily perform his/her duties due to disability or illness.

f) Where an employee is dismissed due to an infraction of Company policy and an injury or illness occurs because of that infraction, benefits will not be payable under the plan.

Accident Compensation: Holiday pay is included within the definition of "earnings as an employee" for the purposes of accident compensation payments. In general terms, an employee who has been absent from work on accident compensation for the fortnight before the holiday, will be paid for the holiday as part of that compensation. However, the employer will be responsible for the holiday pay if the person was at work during the fortnight prior to the accident.

Parental Leave: There is a formula for calculating the public holiday pay entitlement of employees who are absent on parental leave at any time during the fortnight ending on the day of the public holiday. They are entitled to receive one-tenth of an ordinary day's pay, multiplied by the sum of adding together the number of days worked during the fortnight and the number of days during the fortnight on which the employee was absent for reasons unconnected with the parental leave. There is no entitlement to public holiday pay if the employee had not worked at all during the fortnight up to the holiday.

Entitlement:

(a) Female employees

who are eligible for maternity leave or special maternity leave and who apply for and take such leave, will be entitled to receive payment for 6 weeks of maternity leave or special maternity leave, on full pay.

(b) Male employees

who are eligible for paternity leave that apply for and take such leave, will be entitled to receive payment for 6 weeks of paternity leave on full pay.

The paternity leave can be taken in one or two periods, in the following circumstances:

- 2 days at the time of confinement of the employee's spouse (3 days unpaid leave is also available on request); and/or
- a period of 6 weeks (less any paid time taken) in order to be the primary caregiver of a child, where the 6 weeks paid leave is matched with at least an equivalent number of weeks' unpaid leave.

(c) Adoption Leave

An employee who is eligible for adoption leave and who applies for and takes such leave, will be entitled to receive payment for 6 weeks of adoption leave on full pay.

(d) Where both parents are (Company) employees.

Maximum benefit where both parents are (Company) employees, the maximum period of paid parental leave available for any one period of confinement or act of adoption will be six weeks and two days, but which may be taken by either parent or partially by both in a combination of their choice, in accordance with the provisions above.

(e) **Payments**

The 6 weeks Paid Parental Leave benefit is normally paid at the commencement of parental leave and payment is conditional upon return from leave and subsequent completion of 3 months continuous service.

In the event that an employee does not return to work or does not complete 3 months service on return from Parental Leave, they must refund to (Company) the full amount paid in respect of the 6 weeks paid Parental Leave.

As an alternative to this arrangement, employees can elect to defer this payment until 3 months after they return to work. For more information refer to the current Enterprise Agreement.

Voluntary Service: The holiday pay entitlement of an employee on protected voluntary military service is determined in the same way as if the employee had ceased employment at the date on which the service or training commenced.

The Defence Act 1903 and Defence (Re-Establishment) Act 1965 have an overriding effect on Federal and State awards and on industrial agreements. An employee must be allowed leave of absence to attend to his/her defence force obligations. These can include camps and continuous training that seldom exceed 14 days (10 working days) and courses of instruction. The employer must grant leave of absence without pay or if requested leave at credit, to employees who are to attend camps of continuous training. The employee under these circumstances suffers no reduction or bar to the accumulation of other benefits under the award such as sick leave or annual leave. The employee must, if required, produce proof of attendance at camp to the employer. In practice, employees normally receive a letter from their commanding officer requesting attendance for military training.

The Defence (Re-establishment) Act 1965 states that an employer must not hinder a person from volunteering for service in the Emergency Forces or the Reserve Forces or penalise a person on account of their service in these forces.

Jury Service

The term 'jury service' is specific in that it relates to service on a jury or being called to court to serve on a jury even if exempted or rejected from serving. Excluded from jury service would be attendance at court as a litigant or witness.

Where a court hearing is expected to continue for a considerable time, this is usually announced at the beginning of the hearing and employers and employees must make arrangement for this. It is possible to be excused from jury service on the grounds of hardship, but not because of mere inconvenience.

(Company) will pay normal salary for employees attending jury service.

Awards should be checked, as provisions in them tend to vary. The employee is normally obliged to provide proof of attendance, duration of attendance and amount received for attendance. If there is no award provision, there is no obligation to make up pay.

Although the employee will be reimbursed by the Court for his or her attendance, this will usually be less than what s/he would have earned at work. Some awards require employers to make up the balance between jury fees and the ordinary wage.

Emergency Leave

An employee must inform the company if s/he a member of an emergency organisation that may be called to an emergency during working hours. The company consents to the employee attending an emergency during working hours if s/he is obliged to do so as a member of the organisation provided the following conditions have been met:

a) the employee informs the company prior to his or her absence of the reason for the absence and the likely length of the absence;

b) the emergency is within the local jurisdiction of the emergency organisation;

c) the emergency is a declared emergency.

If the employee has been absent from work for two consecutive days and the emergency situation has not abated, the employee must contact the company and the company will decide whether to grant permission to extend the leave of absence. If the employee receives any payment for attending the emergency, that amount will be deducted from the employee's wages for the days absent from work.

Personal Leave:

- personal leave is provided to allow employee's paid time away from the workplace for:
  - o personal illness or injury;
  - o family/household emergency;
  - o death of an immediate family or household member (up to 5 days per event, with further leave at the Supervisor's discretion);
  - o pre-natal medical appointments for prospective parents; and
- with the agreement of the employee's Supervisor, paid personal leave may also be granted for the illness or death of any other relative or close friend of the employee (up to 5 days for each illness or death, with further leave at Supervisor's discretion).

Definitions

Immediate family: is the employee's current or former spouse, de-facto spouse or partner; a child or adult child (including adopted or step-child) parent, grandparent, grandchild or sibling of the employee or of their current or former spouse, de facto spouse or partner.

Family/household emergency: are circumstances that require an employee to care for an immediate family member or to respond to an emergency or unforeseen circumstance that may arise in an employee's personal or domestic situation and which must be responded to personally by the employee. Where reasonable planning can be implemented prior to or in the process of the event, this does not constitute an emergency.

Immediate household: means persons normally resident in the same household as the employee.

Extended Leave without Pay

Leave without Pay (LWOP) is a continuous period of unpaid leave that is granted to an employee by mutual agreement between the employee and the Supervisor and only when it is of mutual benefit to both (Company) and the employee. The same conditions apply as that relating to LWOP under Short-Term Leave without Pay Policy.

Chapter 4

Miscellaneous Human Resources Matters

Hours of Work

Business hours are _____ until _____, unless position determines otherwise.

The following information summarises common provisions found in awards.

The general award provisions have been that ordinary working hours are not to exceed eight hours out of any consecutive 24; 40 hours per week; 120 hours in 21 consecutive days; or 160 hours in 28 consecutive days. It is common for awards to specify shorter standard working hours, i.e.: 35 or 38 hours per week.

Many awards confine the working week from Monday to Friday; however, there is provision in numerous awards that ordinary hours extend from Monday to Sunday.

Work performed outside ordinary or standard hours usually requires payment of 'special or penalty rates,' such as overtime, shift allowances and weekend rates. With the introduction of enterprise bargaining, there has been a development that such payments are not always paid.

Any variation from the above ordinary hours will be set out in the award or agreement, as will rest pauses, meal breaks, gaps between work periods and other matters.

The employer has the right to determine starting and finishing times within limits prescribed in the award or agreement but is usually prohibited from altering them except upon one week's notice. If the employee is a permanent full- or part-time worker, s/he will need to be informed of the prescribed working hours; otherwise, a variation may result in the need to pay penalty rates.

Pay Periods

Pay periods are bi-weekly.

Overtime

Overtime is usually defined as all work performed by an employee for his or her employer outside or in addition to the hours fixed by the award or agreement as 'ordinary hours' of work. Work in excess of the prescribed daily period of work (usually eight hours) must be paid at overtime rates.

The concept of overtime is levied on the employer for requiring an employee to work beyond normal hours. It is also compensation to employees for being required to work the extra hours. For these reasons, overtime payments increase as more hours are worked, in order to cover social inconvenience and lack of rest and leisure time.

It is important to check the overtime clause of the award or agreement to ascertain the following information:

- whether it is payable before a set starting time and/or after a set finishing time;
- whether payable for all time spent travelling home by an employee working unusual hours where no transport is available, and none is provided by the employer;
- provisions regarding meal breaks, i.e.: a break may be due after a certain number of hours and if not taken, overtime is payable until it is.

Meal break provisions during Overtime can also be complex;

- the rate of payment for overtime. The most common rate is at time and one half for the first two hours and double time thereafter;

- any provisions regarding rest periods between completion of overtime and commencement of next work period, 'call back' crib breaks and stand-by payments;
- the effects of any flexible working hours arrangement upon overtime provisions;
- rules and times that apply if ordinary hours are less than 40 per week – i.e.: some industries operate a 35 or 38-hour week;
- any provisions for casual or part-time employees (i.e.: some awards set a maximum standard number of hours for the latter, in which case hours worked in excess of this are treated as overtime), apprentices, junior workers and females (for example.)
- provision of transport). Note that in New South Wales, under the Industrial Relations Act 1996 (sec. 89) a part-time employee is not required to work overtime, although the employer may request them to do so. If overtime is worked, it is paid on the same basis, as it would be for full-time employees. This is a departure from the usual industrial principle that an employer may require an employee to work reasonable overtime.

In most cases, each day's overtime stands alone and cannot be offset on other days. Overtime on weekends generally attracts a higher rate than on weekdays. The wording of the overtime clauses in awards is often very complicated and should be studied carefully. Generally, approval of a Supervisor or supervisor is required before overtime can be worked.

Time in Lieu

If employees are required to work outside their normal hours, time in lieu may be taken. This will be equal to the number of hours worked overtime. Time in lieu is to be taken at a time that is mutually convenient to both parties.

Time in lieu may not be accrued unless agreed with your Department Head. All time in lieu must be taken within a nominated period after the extra hours are worked. Your Department Head will specify this nominated period.

Shift Work

Shift work is work carried on outside the hours normally worked by most employees, namely, the usual 9 to 5, Monday to Friday hours. The basic concept is that another group continues work performed by one group of employees during a shift of eight hours for the following eight hours.

Shifts are commonly of eight hours duration; however, it is becoming more common to have shift spans of 10 or 12 hours. In the case of 12-hour shifts for example, employees may work for 12 hours each day, three days per week.

Change of Status

In the event of change of marital status, a birth or death of a member of the employee's immediate family, change of address or telephone number, s/he is to advise the Human Resources Department, so his/her records can be updated.

Kinds of Employment

1. **Probationary Employees**
   All new employees of (Company) are employed as probationary employees for _____ months, so that their ability to meet the job requirements for the position assigned can be effectively assessed.
2. **Regular Full-time Employees**
   Regular full-time employees are expected to conform to the Company's published hours of work. They may be compensated on an hourly or salaried basis.
3. **Temporary Full-Time and Part-Time Employees**
   May be salaried or paid hourly and have all statutory deductions made. Such temporary employment is not normally for a period of longer than one year. Extensions beyond one year require Department Head's approval.

4. **Contract Personnel**

   Are not employees, but rather are consultants or contractors hired directly by a department with Executive approval. Such individuals or organisations are self-registered with government authorities and are responsible for their own statutory deductions.

5. **Exempt Employees**

   Refers to those employees who are not eligible for overtime pay.

6. **Non-Exempt Employees**

   Refers to those employees who are eligible for overtime pay.

Business Cards

To be provided to all staff on the basis of job requirement. The application for cards should go through the Administration Department and approved by the cost centre Supervisor.

Use of Telephones

It is considered inappropriate to use company phones to make or receive private calls. Therefore, if employees need to make a private phone call during working hours, they will use public phones or their own mobile phones. (Company) realises that in emergency situations employees may need to be notified; however, other private calls while on duty are discouraged. For this reason, Reception will receive all personal incoming calls. Messages from non-urgent personal calls will be placed on the staff notice board. Messages concerning emergency calls will be communicated to employees immediately. Even though many employees have access to extension numbers, they are discouraged from using them to receive private calls.

Salary sacrificing into superannuation fund

Salary sacrifice allows employees to arrange for part of their gross salary to be paid into superannuation. The salary sacrifice amount is paid into their fund, before income tax is deducted, as an additional component of their employer contributions. You can use your (Superannuation Fund) account for salary sacrifice contributions to superannuation.

Consumer protection laws

There are a number of laws such as the Trade Practices Act and the Fair Trading Acts, that are designed to safeguard consumers in their commercial dealings with companies.

These laws prohibit certain types of conduct on the part of companies and their employees. There are three main areas of prohibited conduct that you should be aware of:

- Misleading or Deceptive Conduct;
- False or Misleading Representations; and
- Unconscionable Conduct.

Misleading or Deceptive Conduct

This prohibits companies and their employees from engaging in conduct which is misleading or deceptive or which is likely to mislead or deceive. A simple test to determine what is misleading or deceptive is to ask yourself whether the conduct is truthful and whether it gives a truthful impression. It does not matter that you did not intend to be misleading or deceptive. If your conduct is misleading or deceptive, you may break the law even though you did not intend to. You must take care to ensure that any person you deal with understands what you are saying and that there are always reasonable grounds for you making any statements, promises or predictions.

False or Misleading Representations

This prohibits companies and their employees from making false or misleading representations about their products or services.

You must be very careful when explaining our products to customers and must accurately describe the products and their features. You must not give misleading information, nor suggest that the products have features and benefits they do not have.

If you are unsure of an answer to a customer's question, always advise them that you need to confirm the details and will get back to them. Never guess or assume - and hope you are right.

Unconscionable Conduct

Unconscionable conduct occurs where one party suffers from a special disability or disadvantage, which is taken advantage of by the stronger party.

Accordingly, it is illegal to take advantage of a customer's disadvantage in marketing or selling (Company's) products or services. A person with a "disadvantage" in this context generally means a person who lacks the ability to fully understand the product or service to be provided by (Company) due to such things as illiteracy, lack of education, mental illness, or poor command of English.

The use of unfair tactics or undue pressure in marketing and selling (Company) products or services may also be considered as unconscionable conduct.

IT Systems

Internet/Intranet

(Company) provides Internet and Intranet facilities for staff to communicate and to retrieve or disseminate (Company) and business-related information.

Employees may only use the Internet and Intranet facilities for approved business purposes.

Emails

Emails sent to all staff that do not relate to the business or work will need to be approved by the Supervisor before their release. Employees are discouraged from using the company email system for personal messages and are not to use the company system to search the web unless that search is relevant to work in progress.

(Company) has a policy covering the use of electronic mail. The policy applies to all employees using any (Company) equipment at the workplace, home or remotely.

The electronic email system must be used for business purposes only.

You must not send or receive email or attachments that contain certain things. The policy describes in detail what constitutes unauthorised conduct.

One of the main reasons for restricting the contents of emails is so that (Company) and you as an employee do not incur legal liability. Another reason for restricting email content is to ensure that inappropriate emails do not disrupt the (Company's) IT system or introduce computer viruses.

Software Policy

Employees must ensure that they use only legitimately acquired software and comply with the licensing conditions that apply to that software.

They must not use any software on their computer unless it has been authorised by the (Company's) IT department.

Copyright Policy

Copyright issues arise in many facets of our daily operations. Staff should be cautious before copying or reproducing anything not created within (Company).

For example, copyright may be breached by:

- making copies of documents;
- reproducing another person or company's data in a report; or
- using music or video materials in a training program without permission.

(Company) property declaration

During your employment with (Company) you will be supplied with company property that will assist you in carrying out your responsibilities. You have a duty of care to ensure the items provided are looked after and are not intentionally damaged.

Laptops

Laptops will be provided only for staff involved in travel which requires PC use away from the office for more than 12 times per year. Upon Department Head approval, a laptop will be available from a pool of _____ laptops kept in the Administrative Services Department.

Personal Organisers

Personal Organisers will be supplied to employees after they have obtained Department Head approval.

Mobile Phones

Cellular telephones will be supplied to selected employees with Department Head approval.

Fringe Benefits

Entertainment Expenses

(Company) will subsidise membership in the (Company) Social Club.

All entertainment expenses are approved by the cost centre Supervisor to a maximum of $_____. Department Head must approve expenses above $_____.

Travel Policy

This Travel Policy is aimed at reducing travel expenditures overall and improving the effectiveness of that expenditure.

Discounts are volume based and require compliance where preference is the only decision factor.

Preferred Airline

_____ is the preferred domestic and international airline. Other airlines should be used only when schedule or routing needs can't be met or when a better fare is available.

Class of Travel

All travel is to be Economy Class except for flights in excess of three hours and where circumstances warrant upgrade to business class. This will be managed by exception and must carry approval of the Department Head. Class of travel for international travel over four hours flight time is Business Class.

Ticket Purchase

Advance purchase fares must be used whenever possible, particularly fares that allow upgrade to full economy if the flight schedule changes. Employees are requested to purchase cancellation insurance for every flight.

Accommodation

Preferred hotels must be used. Please contact Corporate Services for more details.

Authorisation

Prior approval of a Department Head is necessary for overseas travel. Travel overseas to be approved by the General Manager. Business Class travel requires the prior approval of a Department Head.

Travel Expenses

This travel policy and procedure is general and is intended to apply to most circumstances. Employees who incur travel expenses during the course of conducting company business are expected to be practical and cost-efficient in their travel practices whenever possible. When possible, travel expenses will be paid directly by employers. Alternative methods of paying travel expenses are:

- specific costs can be met upon presentation of receipts;
- an allowance of a set amount per day or week may be paid to cover incidental extra expenses, in addition to meeting the specific costs;
- the employee can be paid a travel allowance as a component of salary; or
- authority can be given to charge amounts directly to the employer, often using a company credit card.

The latter two methods would be the most convenient where frequent travel is involved. Expense accounts should require the lowest amount of administrative work. Whichever method is selected, employers would be wise to assess the likely amount of travel involved when preparing job descriptions and be able to estimate roughly the cost of this travel.

Companies are encouraged to use Company Travel Agents, especially for overseas travel that would require passports, foreign currency, travellers' cheques and information about overseas countries. CabCharge tickets and cash advances for travel expenses may be obtained upon approval from Administrative Services Department.

- normal air travel is 'economy class.' Employees are to use the lowest applicable airfare by booking the trip in advance whenever possible;
- a car may be rented if necessary, to conduct business in the location to which the employee has travelled and when other means of transportation are unavailable, more costly or impractical. Mid-size vehicles are standard rental. Full-sized cars may be rented when there are more than two occupants;

- employees wishing to utilise their own vehicles for company travel must ensure they have adequate car accident insurance. Reimbursement for business use of a personal automobile is at the rate of ($_____) per kilometre;
- travellers are to book hotels using Company Travel Agent and stay in company-approved hotels. Most hotel reservations are guaranteed, so it's the employee's responsibility to cancel the hotel if it is not going to be used;
- per diem expenses – meal expenses will be as follows: Breakfast ($_____); Lunch ($_____); Dinner ($_____); and
- other allowable expenses are taxis, bus, shuttle, train fare, parking and gratuities.

All expense accounts must be submitted as soon as practicable and not later than the tenth day of the month following the month in which the expenses incurred. All expenses incurred by the employee will be charged to his or her cost centre unless otherwise indicated by the employee. All amounts owing to employees as a result of using their own funds or personal credit cards will be paid within ten (10) working days of submitting expense report.

Subscriptions

Newspapers

Two copies of (name newspapers) will be provided in coffee room for use by all employees. An additional set will be available at the reception desk for reading by waiting guests.

Trade Associations and Union Membership

(Company) encourages staff member to be part of relevant trade association and/or union of their choice. The Human Resources Department will be happy to assist with any advice if requested.

Professional Fees/Subscriptions

Upon completion of their probationary period, employees may request reimbursement of a Union or other professional association related to the work performed. (The maximum amount to be reimbursed is $_____ per person.)

Employment Conditions

Second Jobs

It is the policy of (Company) to allow employees to pursue other opportunities outside the company. This in only provided that the employee meets and continues to meet any and all of their commitments at (Company). Any secondary employment must take second priority to all existing job requirements of (Company).

If at any time involvement in another company is seen as interfering with the interests of (Company) the employee may be asked to terminate such relations or risk further action. All employees will be judged against the same performance standards as other staff members and will be subject to rostering demands as appropriate to the positions. There will be no discrimination against employees pursuing outside interests.

However, an employee is not to be employed or engaged in the conduct of any other business that may compete in any respect with the business of (Company) (except with the written consent of Department Head.)

Coffee, Tea, Smoke Breaks and Lunches

As long as the employee works the required hours, they are allowed two fifteen-minute breaks during their normal workday and one hour for lunch unless otherwise stipulated by rostered hours. Smoke breaks must comply with the allotted break times.

Employment of Relatives

The company may employ relatives of employees, provided they are not employed in the same department. It is the policy of (Company) not to employ relatives of current employees where there may be a conflict of interest or possible breach of confidentiality.

Sign-On Payments/Bonuses

Every incentive or bonus is to be approved in advance by the General Manager.

Use of Company Vehicles

Employees, who have been requested to use the company vehicle, will obtain the keys from the Administrative Services Manager. They will be expected to abide by the rules and laws of the road and will refrain from using the vehicle for personal errands.

- only employees of (Company) will drive or be passengers in company vehicles;
- due to the 'no smoking' policy of (Company) there will be no smoking in company vehicles;
- (Company) will ensure that adequate insurance is placed on the vehicles;
- employee will ensure that gas tank is filled before returning it to the Administrative Services Manager;
- the Administrative Manager will ensure that the vehicle receives regular preventive maintenance and is responsible for ensuring the gas tanks are filled;
- employees who use company vehicle will receive the keys from the Administrative Services Manager;
- employees using the company vehicle must prove that they have a valid driver's licence and immediately notify Administrative Services Manager of any suspensions;
- any traffic violations, such as speeding or illegal parking tickets will be paid by the employee driving the vehicle at the time of the violation;

- any traffic accidents or incidents must be reported to the Administrative Manager when the vehicle is returned; and
- company vehicles will be parked in their designated parking area.

Accepting Gifts

(Company) has developed a policy about accepting gifts and entertainment from contractors and suppliers to our business. The policy affects all (Company) employees.

The policy provides that (Company) employees should not accept gifts, trips entertainment, discounts, loans, commissions or other benefits from contractors or suppliers that might be perceived to influence business decisions.

Set out below are examples of gifts you may and may not accept in connection with your work with (Company).

Acceptable gifts

- ordinary business lunch, dinner or after-work drinks;
- invitations to lunch, dinner or cocktail parties if other company representatives are also present;
- invitations to local sporting events and theatre; or
- invitations to non-local sporting and theatre events where (Company) provides travel, accommodation, and other related expenses.

Unacceptable gifts

- travel, accommodation or meals in connection with any non-local event;
- travel or accommodation provided by a travel agent, airline or hotel as an inducement to future/further service use; or
- any benefits which may be perceived as indicative of favourable treatment, if accepted.

What to do if you are offered unacceptable gifts or benefits

Discuss the situation with the Supervisor of your business unit immediately. Depending on the circumstances, your Supervisor will indicate whether the benefit may be kept by you, kept by (Company) donated to a charity of your choice or returned to the donor. If you have any queries in relation to (Company)'s policy on accepting gifts and entertainment from providers to the business, please contact your Department Head.

Employee Purchases

All employee purchases will be at cost plus 10%. Since this special employee pricing is a privilege, employees are requested that all purchases are for the personal use of the employee and his/her immediate family.

Any employee wishing to make purchases at special employee prices must have an 'Authorisation for Employee Purchase' Form signed by his/her Department Manager and the form is to be taken to the Sales Department where an invoice will be prepared.

The employee will obtain the product and proceed to the Cashier for tendering of the discounted amount.

(Company) Dress Code

To be successful in business, (Company) policy is to dress and behave in a manner that shows respect for both customers and business representatives. This will generally translate into people wearing "corporate casual" as their normal working attire.

Corporate casual clothing is not as formal as business clothing but it still communicates a professional image:

It is: clean, neat, well presented, and comfortable; and

It is not: torn, dirty, faded or clothing with inappropriate or potentially offensive logos or wording.

Some guidelines for Corporate Casual clothing are:

Men:

Clothes:

Collared Tee Shirts
Turtle neck tops
Smart casual shirts
Jumpers/vests/cardigans
Blazers/jackets
Tailored pants/chinos, cords

Shoes:

Boat shoes
Leather Boots (e.g. RM Williams/Doc Martens)
Canvas casual shoes

Women:

Clothes

Shirts/blouses (midriff covered)
Knit tops
Turtle/funnel/cowl/boat neck tops
Twin sets/cardigans/smart casual jumpers
Blazers/jackets
Tailored trousers
Dresses/skirts/tunics (moderate length)

Shoes

Boots
Dress Shoes
Leather sandals
Canvas casual shoes

Some guidelines for Corporate Casual clothing considered *not* appropriate are:

All Employees

- Dying hair unnatural colours

- Ensure that you use perfumes and colognes sparingly
- Torn Jeans
- Refrain from having visible pierced objects other than in the ear.
- Visible display of tattoos and body piercing
- Backless, low-cut or midriff revealing tops
- Flip Flops
- Trainers (Runners)
- Shorts
- Mini-skirts

Work from Home

With today's technology and the nature of certain positions, work can be carried out in the home just as efficiently and effectively as it can be carried out in the office. Management and staff can negotiate flexible work arrangements to best meet an employee's needs, while ensuring that business needs are met.

Work from Home, (WFH) the practice of working at home instead of physically travelling to a central workplace, is a work alternative that (Company) may offer to some employees when it would benefit both the organisation and the employee.

(Company) is committed to providing an environment that supports the use of more flexible work practices through the introduction of company policy and enterprise bargaining initiatives. Such arrangements enhance the career opportunities available to staff through the provision of alternate work arrangements.

WFH is not a formal, universal employee benefit, but is seen as an alternative method of meeting company needs. Because WFH is a privilege, (Company) has the right to refuse to make WFH available to an employee and to terminate a WFH arrangement at any time.

Security

Employees must ensure that all confidential and proprietary information of (Company) is properly secured at all times and that respective work areas are monitored and controlled to prevent access by unauthorised personnel. Employees may not participate in outside business or financial activities that compete with the Company nor use Company assets at any time for personal gain or activity that may compete with the Company. They may not participate in outside business that supplies services or has business dealings with the Company where there is a possibility of preferential treatment being received by virtue of the employee's position.

Emergency Situations

The (Company) Emergency Response Plan is designed to ensure the health and safety of employees and visitors in the event of a fire, bomb threat or first aid emergency. All employees will adhere to the following procedure in the event of an emergency. Floor Wardens are prepared for these emergencies and their names are identified on the bulletin board of each floor.

Fire Evacuation

When the alarm sounds, all occupants shall:

- prepare to evacuate at once;
- leave their work area immediately;
- ensure the doors are left open, in the unlocked position – a Floor Warden will close the door later;
- if away from your normal work area, do not return for any personal belongings;
- walk to the nearest emergency exit (do not use lifts);
- if the alarm stops, continue evacuation unless advised otherwise by fire department personnel;
- assemble at a safe distance from building where the Floor Warden will conduct a head count; and

- Fire Wardens will give additional attention to the evacuation of personnel who are physically disabled.

Bomb Threat and/or Extortion

The person receiving a bomb threat and/or threats of extortion telephone call should remain calm and courteous, not interrupt the caller and try to obtain as much information as possible such as:

- what time will the bomb explode?
- what does the bomb look like and where is it?
- identification of the caller – what does his/her voice sound like, is it soft or harsh, male or female, accents, etc.

Record the details of the conversation and notify the Chief Floor Warden. Do not activate the fire alarm.

Employees may evacuate if they so desire but are not required to do so until they are advised to leave by the Floor Warden. If evacuation is requested, employees should gather up their personal parcels, purses, briefcases, etc. and follow the instructions of the Floor Warden.

Medical Emergency

Make a quick assessment of the situation to determine the nature of the medical emergency. Have someone notify a Floor Warden of the emergency and if the situation dictates, phone 000 requesting medical assistance giving address and description of the injury.

The responding Floor Warden will apply appropriate emergency first aid until medical assistance or paramedics arrive.

The Supervisor of the employee will investigate the incident, inform WorkCover and complete a 'Reporting of an Incident/Hazard/Near Miss' report.

Chapter 5

Discrimination and Harassment

Equal Employment Opportunity (EEO)

(Company) is committed to providing all employees with an atmosphere of dignity and mutual respect, one on which they are judged solely on criteria related to job performance. It is (Company)'s policy to maintain a work environment that is free from discrimination or harassment.

(Company) will make this known to all employees through training and/or in the case of new employees, as part of their induction.

Definition of Employment in EEO Legislation

The term 'employment' in the EEO legislation includes:

- recruitment and selection;
- promotion and transfer;
- training and development; and
- conditions of employment.

Federal EEO Legislation

Federal government legislation makes it illegal to discriminate on the grounds of:

- sex;
- marital status;
- pregnancy;
- race (including colour, nationality or ethnic origin);
- disability; or
- family responsibilities.

State EEO Legislation

Some states have additional EEO legislation that makes it unlawful to:

- Discriminate on the grounds of:
  - religious or political beliefs;
  - physical and intellectual impairment;
  - sexuality (i.e.: homosexuality);
  - parenthood, either being a parent or childless;
  - age; or
  - trade union activity;
- engage in racial vilification; or
- incite racial or religious hatred.

Sexual Harassment/Discrimination

(Company) is to maintain a work environment free from unlawful discrimination and harassment. It is the right of each employee to be treated with dignity and respect and it is each employee's responsibility to treat others the same way.

(Company) will not tolerate sexual harassment in any form. Sexual Harassment is unlawful. It amounts to discriminatory behaviour under Federal and State anti-discrimination legislation. This responsibility extends not only to employees, but also to all people with whom we deal in conducting our business. Any such inappropriate behaviour will be taken very seriously.

Sexual Harassment is a form of discrimination that occurs when a person is subjected to unwelcome, uninvited behaviour they find offensive, humiliating, embarrassing, or intimidating. It can take many forms and may include physical contact, verbal comments, jokes, pictures and gestures. It includes many things that might not readily be perceived as sexual harassment by everyone, but which the law says amounts to sexual harassment and/or discrimination. These include:

- repeated, unwanted comments about a person's religious or political beliefs;
- unwanted name calling;
- distribution or display of material regarded as offensive;

54

- persistent questions about a person's private life;
- jokes, suggestive comments, pictures or offensive gestures related to a person's disability, religious conviction, or ethnic or sexual characteristics;
- repeated, unwanted, and deliberate physical contact;
- indecent assault or other similar criminal offences; and
- repeated requests for dates.

Employees found to have committed acts of sexual harassment will be subject to disciplinary action that may include warnings or dismissal.

(Company) has a legal obligation to take 'all reasonable steps' to prevent discrimination and harassment occurring in the company. The company is ensuring that all employees clearly understand what harassment is by introducing an ongoing education program. All managers and supervisors must reinforce the message to their staff that harassment in any form is not acceptable and that any victimisation of those who speak against it will not be tolerated.

Sexual harassment can take many forms and may include physical contact or intimacy, verbal comments, jokes, pictures, propositions or the display of offensive material and other behaviour that creates an uncomfortable or sexually hostile environment. It may occur as a single incident and/or a series of incidents.

Sexual harassment is not behaviour that is based on mutual attraction, friendship and respect. Consent must be something positively given and the relevant behaviour welcomed or reciprocated. (Company) has no intention of intruding into individual workplace relationships, which are consensual and based on mutual respect.

Objectives

(Company) is committed to a comprehensive strategy for eliminating discrimination and harassment. We aim to:

- create an environment where all employees and customers are treated with dignity, courtesy and respect;
- implement training and awareness raising strategies to ensure that all employees know their rights and responsibilities;
- provide an effective procedure for complaints based on the principles of natural justice;
- treat all complaints in a sensitive, fair, timely and confidential manner;
- provide protection from victimisation or reprisals;
- encourage the reporting of behaviour which breaches this policy; and
- promote appropriate standards of conduct at all times.

Workplace Bullying, Harassment and Violence

[Unfortunately, Australia does not have specific laws that protect employees against workplace bullying, harassment and violence. Most countries have a section in their Occupational Health and Safety laws that cover those offenses, but they are not covered in any of the federal or state Occupational Health and Safety laws in Australia.

In Australia, estimates of harassment in the workplace range from 400,000 to two million workers affected each year! This affects up to five million workers at some point during their working lives (Beyond Bullying Association 2001). With a total Australian population of 22.68 million people and over 11.5 million people in the workplace - this is not a problem - it's an epidemic!

Bullying costs the Australian economy up to $13 Billion a year in absenteeism, compensation, management time and lost productivity. 1,100 Victorian claims for compensation because of workplace violence, harassment and bullying cost $26 Billion. Half of workplaces employ bullies and up to half of all workers will be bullied at least once during their careers.

Every Australian Human Resources Manager should be lobbying the Australian government to implement laws (not simply *'Codes of Ethics'* or *'Guidance Notes,')* but **laws** that have 'teeth' to protect Australian employees.

However, in the interim your company could implement its own workplace bullying policies and procedures to cover this omission and ensure that those policies are very clear that workplace bullying, harassment and violence will not be tolerated within your company.

Sample (Company) Bullying, Harassment and Violence Policy

(Company name's) policy and practice is to maintain a work environment free from unlawful discrimination and harassment. It is the right of each employee to be treated with dignity and respect and it is each employee's responsibility to treat others the same way.

(Company name) will not tolerate offensive, humiliating, coercive, intimidating, or harassing behaviour from anyone. This responsibility extends not only to employees, but also to all people with whom we deal in conducting our business. Any such inappropriate behaviour will be taken very seriously.

(Company's) Objectives

(Company) is committed to a comprehensive strategy for eliminating workplace bullying, harassment, and violence. We aim to:

- Create an environment where all employees and customers are treated with dignity, courtesy and respect;
- Implement training and awareness raising strategies to ensure that all employees know their rights and responsibilities;
- Provide an effective procedure for complaints based on the principles of natural justice;
- Provide protection from victimisation or reprisals;

- Treat all complaints in a sensitive, fair, timely and confidential manner;
- Encourage the reporting of behaviour which breaches this policy; and
- Promote appropriate standards of conduct at all times.

Definitions:

Harassment includes many things that might not readily be perceived as harassment by everyone, but which the law says amounts to harassment. These include:

- Belittling, demeaning or patronising the victim - especially in front of others;
- Shouting at and threatening the target, often in front of others;
- Making snide comments to see if the person will fight back;
- Finding fault and criticising everything the victim says and does or twisting, distorting and misrepresenting the victim. The criticism may be of a trivial nature; but often there's a grain of truth in it that can dupe the victim into believing the criticism is valid.
- Stubbornly refuse to recognise the victim's contributions;
- Attempting to chip away at the target's status, self-confidence, worth and potential;
- Treating the victim differently - showing favouritism to others and bias toward the victim.

Application of Policy

This policy applies to all activities and all people involved in those activities (whether or not they are (Company's) employees that take place:

- On (Company name) premises and
- Otherwise as a consequence of employment at (Company name).

Chapter 6

Employee Assistance Program

(Company) recognises that the challenges of today's demanding business environment, along with the demands experienced in one's personal or family life, can significantly affect one's overall well-being. When an employee's well-being is affected, so is their work performance and job satisfaction.

Because of this, (Company) has introduced the Employee Assistance Program, which supports employees to deal effectively with troublesome issues at home or work. When the individual has an opportunity to discuss these difficult issues with someone, their home life and work productivity improves, and everyone benefits.

Your EAP is a professional, confidential counselling and consultative advice service provided for you by (Counselling Company); a private firm specialising in employee assistance programs.

(Counselling Company's) counsellors are all experienced professionals who have extensive training in counselling and workplace consulting. The EAP aims to:

- assist staff to manage the demands of their jobs;
- help them resolve personal issues which may be affecting their work performance;
- increase their overall well-being; and
- help them to achieve peak performance levels.

Who can use the EAP?

All employees of (Company). Immediate family members or people in close relationships with them may accompany an employee.

How confidential is the EAP?

(Company) is not provided with the names of employees who use the EAP service, and any information provided to (Company) is non-identifying.

(Counselling Company) treats all EAP consultations as confidential and does not share information about staff unless authorised by the employee in writing.

Do I have to pay for the EAP?

The EAP is free of charge for the first _____ sessions. Most people find that within that time they can clarify the issue, develop an action plan and start moving towards solving their problems.

If employees find they'd like further assistance, they can negotiate to extend the service at their own cost, or the counsellor can refer them on to another service appropriate to their needs. Every effort is made to recommend a service that is either free, covered by health insurance or has a fee scale based on the employee's ability to pay.

Chapter 7

Employee Discipline

This policy establishes the disciplinary procedures to be followed in cases of misconduct or poor performance. It is designed to ensure that these procedures are in accordance with legislative standards and principles of natural justice. It applies to all employees of (Company).

Probationary Employees

Probationary employees are excluded from the coverage of the federal termination of employment law, provided the probationary period is determined in advance and if it is longer than three months - is reasonable in the circumstances.

Probationary periods are viewed as similar to a fixed term contract, so that the contract of employment comes to an end. Provided the employee is found to be satisfactory, a new contract of employment is then entered into. Thus, an employer can dismiss an employee (i.e.: refuse to offer further employment) at the end of a probationary period, without the employee having any legal redress. Notice should be given so that it expires before the end of the probationary period.

Probationary employees can also be dismissed prior to the expiry of the probationary period unless there is a contractual term or understanding between the parties (i.e.: an oral term in the contract of employment) to the contrary.

Types of Disciplinary Action

Depending on the seriousness of the matter, disciplinary action can take various forms:

- counselling interview;
- written warning – Initial;
- written warning - Further:

- written warning – Final;
- suspension and dismissal;
- dismissal with notice; or
- summary dismissal without notice

Type of Action: Counselling Interview.
Kind of Behaviour: Minor Misconduct.
Steps taken: Disciplinary warning template completed and signed by all parties. Copy kept by employee, Supervisor and put on personnel file. If there is a union – they also get a copy.
Who takes action: Employee's Supervisor.

Type of Action: First Written Warning.
Kind of Behaviour:
(1) Misconduct of a more serious nature;
(2) Previous counselling or verbal warning for same or similar matter.
Steps taken: Disciplinary warning template completed and signed by all parties. Copy kept by employee, Supervisor and put on personnel file. If there is a union – they also get a copy.
Who takes action: Employee's Supervisor and Observer.

Type of Action: Further Written Warning.
Kind of Behaviour: Similar to first written warning. Used where there has been a previous written warning.
Steps taken: Disciplinary warning template completed and signed by all parties. Copy kept by employee, Supervisor and put on personnel file. If there is a union – they also get a copy.
Who takes action: Employee's Supervisor and Observer.

Type of Action: Final Written Warning.
Kind of Behaviour: Serious Misconduct or failure to comply with previous written warning. Used to warn that further misconduct may lead to dismissal.
Steps taken: Disciplinary warning template completed and signed by all parties. Copy kept by employee, Supervisor and put on personnel file. If there is a union – they also get a copy.
Who takes action: Employee's Supervisor and Observer.

Type of Action: Suspension.

Kind of Behaviour: Pending the completion of an investigation of alleged Serious Misconduct.

Steps taken: Disciplinary warning template completed and signed by all parties. Copy kept by employee, Supervisor and put on personnel file. If there is a union – they also get a copy.

Who takes action: Department Head (or delegate) with approval of Human Resources Manager and Legal Counsel.

Type of Action: Termination with Notice.

Kind of Behaviour: Serious Misconduct.

Steps taken: Interview tape recorded. Disciplinary warning template completed and signed by all parties. Copy kept by employee, Supervisor and put on personnel file. If there is a union – they also get a copy.

Who takes action: Department Head (or delegate) with approval of Human Resources Manager and Legal Counsel.

Type of Action: Summary Dismissal without Notice.

Kind of Behaviour: Serious Misconduct.

Steps taken: Interview tape recorded. Disciplinary warning template completed and signed by all parties. Copy kept by employee, Supervisor and put on personnel file. If there is a union – they also get a copy.

Who takes action: Department Head (or delegate) with approval of Human Resources Manager and Legal Counsel.

Counselling Interview

If the interview is for a minor problem, (possibly the employee wasn't aware of a company policy) a counselling interview is called for. The employee and Supervisor keep a copy of the documentation. This documentation is not placed on the employee's personnel file in Human Resources unless the situation continues.

Written Warning - Initial

When the misconduct is of a more serious nature or if there has already been a counselling and/or verbal warning given to the employee on the same or similar matter and the problem has not been rectified within the time stipulated on earlier interviews, then a disciplinary warning is used to document the proceedings.

Written Warning - Further

In some cases where a First Written Warning has been given, a Further Written Warning may be given rather than a Final Written Warning.

The procedure for a Further Written Warning is similar to that used for a First Written Warning.

Written Warning - Final

When the misconduct is of a more serious nature or if there has already been a recent disciplinary warning on file regarding the same or similar misconduct, then a final disciplinary warning is used to document the proceedings.

Suspension and Dismissal

This type of disciplinary action is dealt with in a later section of this policy.

In matters of the most serious misconduct or following a further instance of misconduct after a final written warning has been placed on employee's file, then it may be appropriate to dismiss the employee with notice.

Once a decision to dismiss an employee has been made by the employee's Department Head, this will be confirmed in writing to the employee.

Where inquiries are being made into misconduct that:

- is serious enough that it may result in dismissal;
- the employee's responses need to be considered or further investigated; and
- it is inappropriate that the employee remains in the workplace; the employee should be suspended on full pay following approval.

Supervisors will ensure that there is no undue delay in finalising the matter following the suspension of an employee.

Serious Misconduct

For the purposes of this document, Serious Misconduct is defined as:

- wilful, or deliberate behaviour by a employee that is inconsistent with the continuation of the contract of employment; or
- conduct that causes imminent, and serious risk to:
    1. the health and safety of a person; or
    2. the reputation, viability or profitability of (Company)'s business.

Serious Misconduct includes, but is not limited to:

1. possession of, or trafficking of illegal drugs on company premises;
2. consuming alcohol or illegal drugs on company premises, except where alcohol is specifically authorised for a social function by a Department Head;
3. reporting for, or returning from breaks or company appointments, under the influence of alcohol;
4. possession of unauthorised weapons on company premises;
5. theft;
6. fraud;
7. dishonesty;
8. breach of customer confidentiality;
9. unauthorised use of (Company) information, systems or other assets;
10. sexual harassment;
11. discrimination;
12. physical assault;
13. harassment or bullying;

14. deliberate destruction of (Company) property; or

15. engaging in sexual activities on company premises.

Termination

An employee cannot be terminated:

- by way of a 'forced' resignation with dismissal as the only alternative;
- for a temporary absence from work due to illness or injury;
- on grounds that may be regarded as discriminatory – i.e.: race, gender, age, sexuality, religion, union membership etc.

In cases of Serious Misconduct, summary dismissal without notice may be appropriate.

Interviews that may result in dismissal

When arranging a disciplinary interview where a possible outcome of that interview is termination of employment, the employee should be advised that:

- they have the right to arrange for an independent person of their choosing to be present during the interview; and
- the matter is viewed very seriously by (Company) and in the case of Serious Misconduct, may result in termination of employment.

Chapter 8

Grievance Handling

(Company) aims to provide an effective and acceptable means for employees to bring grievances concerning their work and their well-being at work to the attention of management staff. With that in mind, a formal grievance handling procedure has been established for the benefit of all staff to ensure that all grievances are satisfactorily resolved.

Please note that this is directed specifically at workplace grievances that do not involve Discrimination and Harassment. Where a complaint involves Discrimination or Harassment, refer to the document entitled, 'Eliminating Discrimination and Harassment.'

(Company) is committed to ensuring that all grievances are handled, impartially, free from repercussions, quickly and with discretion.

A grievance is any type of problem, concern or complaint related to work or the work environment. A grievance may be about any act, omission, situation or decision that is considered unfair, discriminatory of unjustified.

Confidentiality

(Company) is committed to ensuring that all complaints are treated impartially, fairly, confidentially, and promptly. (Company) considers confidentiality to be one of the most important aspects in dealing with a complaint. It is important to respect the rights of all parties, particularly during an investigation. No confidential information will be divulged to anyone who is not directly involved in the complaint or the investigation of it.

A request for confidentiality (such as keeping confidences and not taking any action) by any employee who discusses a problem with a fellow employee, will be seriously considered.

(Company) must take appropriate steps however, to investigate and resolve the grievance. Any investigation/resolution will be handled with the utmost discretion.

(Company) recognises, in some circumstances, individuals may wish to nominate a work colleague or independent counsellor as a support person during the grievance process. This nominated person must also respect the need for confidentiality.

However, guarantees of confidentiality in every situation cannot be given. There may be circumstances where information given cannot be kept in confidence, such as when physical violence or criminal activity is alleged or when (Company) must investigate allegations by talking to other individuals. Direct action will be taken to protect the individual while resolving the issue. The investigation will be discussed in detail with the employee throughout the process.

Documents used in the handling of a complaint will remain confidential even after the complaint has been resolved. The Human Resources Department will store documents securely.

In accessing the grievance procedure, individuals must understand that (Company) will exercise utmost discretion and require confidentiality to the extent practicable. As disclosure of information relating to a complaint can damage reputations and result in defamation, (Company) sees a breach of discretion by any party during an investigation as a serious issue. Management will deal with offenders appropriately.

Breaches of Confidentiality during an Investigation

The Human Resources Manager will immediately deal with any employee who breaches confidentiality or discusses an incident while an investigation is under way.

Staff involved will be informed of the consequences of their action, both in terms of the investigation (i.e.: making the grievance harder to resolve) and their own situation (i.e.: they could be subject to disciplinary action).

The Complainant must be informed about the breach of confidentiality and asked what action they would like taken.

Employees who have been given information about the investigation will be advised not to discuss the incident. They will also be warned that continued discussion about the incident could further damage the investigation and will result in disciplinary action being taken.

The right of appeal

Where either the person lodging the complaint or the individual whose conduct is complained about believes that the process of hearing a grievance has not followed the procedures outlined in this policy, and/or they are dissatisfied with the final outcome, they can appeal the decision.

The appeal should be in writing and delivered to the Human Resources Manager within 14 days of delivery of the decision that is appealed against. The Human Resources Manager will arrange for the appropriate Department Head or a representative of Human Resources who have not been associated with the case to review:

- the way in which the case was handled; and
- the procedures that were followed.

They will then recommend an appropriate course of action.

It is the responsibility of the Human Resources Manager to implement any disciplinary action.

It is (Company's) legal obligation to investigate all complaints, whether they have been brought to its attention formally or informally. All employees are assured that investigations will be guided by the principles of integrity and confidentiality and that an employee will not be treated less favourably or detrimentally because they have lodged a complaint.

At all times, a Complainant's preferred means of resolution will guide the complaints handling process.

Chapter 9

Occupational Health and Safety

It is the aim of (Company) to minimise the risk of injury and disease to employees and other persons by adopting a planned and systematic approach to the management of occupational health, safety and welfare and providing the resources for its successful implementation.

An objective of the Occupational Health and Safety Act 1985 is the elimination, at the source, of risks to the health, safety and welfare of persons at work. Some regulations supporting the act provide specific directions relating to risk control (i.e.: Noise regulations). Elimination of risk is required wherever practicable. (Company) will achieve its occupational health, safety and welfare objectives by developing and implementing appropriate policies and procedures which document standards and guide managers, supervisors and employees to carry out their responsibilities.

Occupational Health and Safety Coordinator

The Occupational Health and Safety Coordinator has responsibility to coordinate (Company's) management of health and safety on behalf of the Responsible Officer. The Occupational Health and Safety Coordinator does not assume the responsibilities of managers and supervisors.

The Occupational Health and Safety Coordinator has a responsibility to:

- coordinate the identification, development, implementation and review of health and safety-related policies and procedures;
- assist managers and supervisors in the identification, assessment and selection of measures to control hazards and risks to health and safety;

- assist managers and supervisors in monitoring and evaluating hazards and risk control measures;
- monitor and advise on legislative and technical changes to health and safety;
- assist managers and supervisors in the identification, development and provision of appropriate health and safety-related information, instruction and training;
- monitor and provide regular reports to the Responsible Officer and the Health and Safety Committee on (Company's) occupational health and safety performance; support employees to follow policies and develop safe work procedures.

Health and Safety Committees

(Company) has established a Health and Safety Committee consisting of management and employee representatives. This committee will be the principal forum where management consults with employees on broad health and safety policy issues. It will ensure that Occupational Health and Safety representatives are appointed to monitor and ensure compliance with the safety procedures of the company.

Health and Safety Representatives

Health and Safety Representatives (HSRs) are elected by (Company) employees for a two-year term and represent employees relating to health and safety matters. It is expected that after the initial training, there will be an average time commitment of up to 2 hours per month.

HSRs are elected to represent the Designated Workgroup (DWG) in which they work. Training in health and safety procedures is provided to assist HSRs to carry out their roles.

HSRs are responsible for facilitating health and safety awareness and resolving health and safety matters in a prompt manner through direct consultation with relevant parties. They act as a contact point and champion for all employees in their DWG for health and safety matters.

Employee Responsibilities:

- follow safe working procedures and instructions, ensuring that safe work practices are undertaken in the workplace;
- report any health and safety concerns, incidents or hazards to their Supervisor and/or HSR;
- assist in the identification of hazards, the assessment of risks and the implementation of risk control measures;
- obey any reasonable instruction aimed at protecting their health and safety while at work; and
- ensure that they are not affected by alcohol or another drug, which may endanger their own, or any other person's health and safety.

What is a hazard?

A hazard is any situation with the potential to cause injury or illness, or, in the case of dangerous goods, damage to property. Some examples of hazards are:

- airborne contaminants (fumes, dusts, fibres);
- noise;
- manual handling (lifting, carrying, pushing);
- dangerous chemicals or harmful substances;
- operating machinery; and
- moving vehicles.

Smoke Free Workplace Policy

(Company) is committed to ensuring a safe, healthy, and efficient work environment exists for our people and all visitors to our workplace. In line with this commitment (Company) has adopted a smoke-free workplace policy.

Smokers will adhere to the coffee and lunch break times allowed by all employees. There are to be no additional smoke breaks.

Smoking is not permitted on (Company) premises. These premises include any property used by the company for conducting business, including branch offices and office buildings.

Smokers are not to smoke outside the main entrances of (Company) premises. All people need to be able to enter a (Company) workplace without being exposed to passive smoking risks. For safety reasons, smoking in loading bays and outside car park entrances is not permitted.

Anyone wishing to smoke during working hours must use normal tea/coffee and lunch breaks times to do so.

In any circumstance where this policy is infringed, the Supervisor of the individual or the Supervisor responsible for the individual's presence in the workplace will act in accordance with (Company's) policy and guidelines. Breaches of (Company) policies will result in disciplinary action, which may include termination of employment.

[As mentioned earlier, in many countries, the Occupational Health and Safety Act also covers Workplace Bullying, Harassment and Violence, but this is not included in any of Australia's relevant Acts.]

Chapter 10

Performance Appraisals

Employees of (Company) will receive a Performance Appraisal two weeks before their probation period ends and once a year thereafter.

Shortly after an employee is hired, the employee and Supervisor carefully review the employee's Position Description. The Supervisor will complete Part 1 of the 'Probationary Performance Appraisal' Form and discuss the contents with the employee. A copy of the employee's position description is attached to the Performance Appraisal Form.

During this probationary period Supervisors will check to see if the new employee requires clarification or help in completing his/her duties. Supervisors are expected to guide and train employees and be available for any questions employees might have about the requirements of their positions. Two weeks before the employee's probationary period is to end, the Supervisor will conduct a Performance review and go over the contents with the employee. At this time it should be apparent whether the Supervisor wishes to keep the employee on staff or to terminate them. If the employee's performance is unacceptable, the Supervisor will begin the termination process. A copy of the employee's Performance Appraisal outlining the unacceptable behaviour will be placed on the personnel file in the Human Resources Department and the termination paperwork will be completed.

If the employee's performance is acceptable, s/he becomes a permanent employee of the company and a copy of the completed Performance Appraisal is placed on the employee's personnel file. At the time the employee is hired, it should be determined whether the employee will receive a salary increase upon successful completion of his/her probationary period (optional).

Within the next two weeks, the Supervisor will complete the Performance Appraisal Form for the next appraisal period. There are three ways the Supervisor can set the time for the next appraisal period;

- appraisal period can be conducted yearly where all employees are evaluated at the same time (not recommended);
- appraisal period can be done on the anniversary date of when the employee began working for the company (preferred); and/or
- appraisal period can be used for special projects where the employee is evaluated on how well s/he completes a project.

Chapter 11

Re-deployment and Redundancy

When does Redundancy apply?

Where an employee's position no longer exists (Company's) immediate priority will be to re-deploy that individual. Where an individual in a redundant position can be re-deployed into a position that is at least an equivalent role, redundancy will not apply. Where re-deployment efforts are unsuccessful, redundancy provisions will apply.

It is important to remember that it is a position that is made redundant, rather than a specific individual.

In order to optimise the retention of key staff, (Company) will not operate a voluntary redundancy policy.

Key Principles

The following key principles will apply during the process of redundancy.

- employees facing redundancy will be treated with respect, dignity and care;
- every effort will be made to re-deploy people into suitable roles;
- the Re-deployment search period may be up to 4 weeks;
- short term Re-deployment options as well as any longer-term options will be explored;
- Supervisors are responsible for successfully managing people whose positions become redundant;
- Employees, Supervisors and the Human Resources Manager will be jointly responsible for seeking alternative roles;
- Employees advised they are on Re-deployment will be given an opportunity to raise any suggestions or

comments as to re-deployment options available to them;

- employees advised of redundancy will be offered career transition, financial and personal counselling;
- where no short- or long-term options exist, the individual will receive redundancy benefits.
- (Company) has an obligation to inform the union of any proposed retrenchments. The Human Resources Manager manages redundancy.

Re-deployment is the process whereby active attempts are made to find a suitable role that is equivalent to an individual's skills: experience, capabilities and remuneration level should the employee's position become redundant. If a suitable role is found then the individual will be expected to accept this role. If an employee refuses a suitable role then resignation would apply.

Re-deployment will occur when an individual has been advised that they have not been successful for a role and their current role no longer exists. Employees, who do not express an interest in any role, where their current role no longer exists, will automatically move into the Re-deployment process.

Employees, who are advised that redundancy is a probability, will be able to commence a career transition program.

Options:

Career Counselling

a. Career counselling will be available in-house from (Company) Human Resources Manager. This counselling involves the completion of several career counselling questionnaires. The employee will receive the following:
   i. list of 20 primary and 20 secondary occupations that would use their existing skills and abilities;
   ii. identify their transferable skills;

    iii. determine what they think their abilities are - compared to what they really are;

    iv. whether they have 'what it takes' to become an entrepreneur;

    v. a psychological report that includes:

- their strengths in the areas of interest, ability, values, personality and capacity;
- determine their management, persuasive, social, artistic, clerical, mechanical, investigative and operational abilities
- whether they are outgoing, reserved, factual, creative, analytical, caring organised or casual;
- their ability to think, reason, and solve problems; and their IQ score.

Or:

b. The following career transition programs are available through (Recruitment Company).

    i. Level 1 is an open-ended program for total package levels above $_____.

    ii. Level 2 is a 16-week program for salary and total package levels $_____ to $_____.

    iii. Level 3 is a 6-week program for salary levels up to $_____.

Employee Assistance Program

(Counselling Company) will provide personal counselling to any employee or immediate family member requiring this kind of support. In accordance with current policy, after their final date of termination, employees who have left the organisation may access this facility for a period of up to 6 months.

Employee Accepts Lower Graded Position

If there is no position available in the company that is at the same grade level, but there is one at a lower level, the employee can either accept the company redundancy package or accept the lower-level graded position.

What if an individual declines a re-deployment?

If an individual refuses a permanent or project role that is equivalent to their existing role in terms of remuneration, use of skills, capabilities, and experience, then resignation would apply.

What happens if an individual is re-deployed into a short-term role?

If an individual was re-deployed into a short-term role (6 weeks or less) redundancy would apply at the conclusion of the period, unless both parties agree for the individual to be re-deployed into a permanent or project role.

Immediate Termination

There will be some instances when redundancy is confirmed for an individual and it will be imperative for the company that they exit on the same day. This will be a decision made by the Supervisor and will require the approval of the appropriate Department Head.

With immediate departures, the same benefits are available to the individual; however, his/her redundancy documentation will be couriered to his/her home.

Reference Letters

A certificate of service is provided as part of the redundancy kit. (Company) will provide departing staff with a reference on official company letterhead that reflects their performance with the company. Supervisors may give staff a personal reference if they wish on company letterhead.

Employees Absent on Leave

Employees on parental leave, leave without pay, extended sick leave or disability leave will not be made redundant while on leave. If their role has been made redundant while they were on leave, re-deployment efforts will commence prior to their returning to work. Special cases may be referred to the Human Resources Manager.

Re-Employment after Redundancy

Permanent re-employment after redundancy may occur (except where less than one year has elapsed since retrenchment or the employee's redundancy pay is still in effect) if the individual is clearly the best possible candidate for a position.

The approval of the Human Resources Manager will also be required in all cases of permanent re-employment.

Redundancy Payments Policy

The individual will receive a kit that explains the calculations, tax treatment, superannuation entitlement and options, outplacement, and Employee Assistance Program at the time they are advised of the redundancy.

Chapter 12

Relocation

The overriding principle governing the relocation of an employee is that the company will meet reasonable expenses that necessarily arise because of relocating an employee at the company's request. The company will seek to mitigate the cost of transfers and will endeavour to ensure the employee is not disadvantaged.

This policy relates to permanent relocations, where an employee is permanently transferred (period of more than 12 months) to another location at the company's request.

1.1 Letter of Appointment.

All employees relocating on a temporary basis are to receive a letter outlining the terms and conditions of the temporary transfer. This letter should also include the position and accountabilities, the commencement date and duration of the transfer. Employees are required to formally accept the offer of temporary transfer.

The Supervisor responsible for the temporary transfer should discuss the terms and conditions of the transfer with the employee to ensure there is no misunderstanding and to enable the employee to raise any issues that may need to be taken into consideration. Generally, the minimum length of temporary transfer is six months.

2. Terms and Conditions for Permanent Relocations (longer than 12 months).

The company will reimburse incidental expenses arising because of the temporary relocation, such as any costs associated with the termination of lease on existing property.

These expenses do not include general living expenses such as food.

2.1 Pre-move visit.

A pre-move visit to the new location for the employee and his/her partner/family will be made available once the employee has agreed in principle to relocating.

The aim of the pre-visit is to:

- commence the process of searching for a suitable area and home in which to live;
- investigate schools;
- familiarise employee and his/her family with the new city; and
- enable the employee to visit the new work location.

Pre-visits are to be managed by one of the following relocation companies:

- ....
- ....
- ....

2.2 Relocation Expense reimbursements.

Up to $_____ in transfer induced expenses may be reimbursed (receipts provided) on approval of the employees' Supervisor. This is to cover costs such as buying new school uniforms, refitting curtains, changing over drivers' licenses and car registration, altering plumbing and electrical outlets or other unavoidable costs directly attributable to the transfer.

2.3 Transfer Allowance.

A transfer allowance of $_____ for employee and $_____ for partner, with an additional $_____ per dependant is payable upon the date of transfer. This allowance is designed to assist with incidental costs incurred as a result of relocating.

This payment is gross payment and will be paid through payroll, upon advice by the new Supervisor.

2.4 Career Planning for Spouse.

The company will provide career-planning support for the partner of the employee relocating. Career counselling will be available in-house from the Human Resources Manager before or after the employee re-locates.

2.5 Travel Costs.

The company will pay an allowance (net equivalent) of the cost of one economy airfare for each member of the household transferring to the new location.

If the employee chooses to drive, s/he will be paid the equivalent of the airfares (one month pre-purchase) to cover all costs associated with travelling to the new location.

2.6 Leave associated with the transfer.

Up to 8 days paid leave is available to cover travel time, packing and unpacking and pre-move visit. This leave may be taken in one period or more than one period and is to be negotiated with the employee's new Supervisor.

2.7 Transfer Accommodation

This is accommodation that is needed to assist the employee prior to moving into their permanent accommodation.

Up to 17 days paid accommodation for all transfer needs is available. This includes pre-move visit accommodation and new location accommodation. The employee can select a hotel from the preferred listing and where the stay is likely to be longer than 3 nights - serviced apartments must be considered.

Where there are no kitchen facilities available, all reasonable costs for meals will be reimbursed.

Where there are no laundry facilities and the stay is longer than 3 days, the company will reimburse reasonable laundry costs.

2.8 Emergency Travel.

In the event of an emergency an employee may apply for up to 2 flights back to his/her original location during the first 2 years of transfer. This is to be used for emergencies only for unplanned events such as the illness of a close relative, death in the family, problems with owned property etc. Approval is at Supervisor's discretion.

2.9 Removal.

The company will pay all reasonable costs for removal of the employee's furniture, furnishing and normal household items, including packing and insurance.

A maximum of two cars is included in the cost.

Removal costs may include transferring two family pets. Any additional pets are to be paid for by the employee.

One of the preferred suppliers (Relocation Provider) is to be used.

All communication relating to the removal of the goods such as collection and delivery times and addresses is to be managed by the employee.

Cleaning of vacated premises is the responsibility of the employee and any costs associated with cleaning existing vacated premises will not be covered by (Company).

2.10 Insurance.

Insurance is to be arranged through a preferred supplier and administered through outsourced vendor.

2.11 Storage.

The company will pay the costs of storage of furniture for up to 4 months from the date of transfer that will be managed through the outsource vendor.

3. Permanent and or pre-purchase Accommodation.

Employees are encouraged to make decisions about permanent accommodation as soon as possible.

Employees may be provided with assistance in finding suitable accommodation using the services of a relocation provider. (See 4.1 for levels of relocation services and entitlements).

3.1 Employees selling own home and buying new home in new location.

The company will pay rental assistance to employees who relocate on a temporary basis. Rental assistance is to be based on no loss/no gain principle and is to be provided for accommodation that is comparable in terms of size and location to the old location. Where no rental gap subsidy applies, it will be paid in the form of a Living Away from home Allowance and will not be subject to FBT.

(Company) will pay the costs associated with the sale of employee's own home and the purchase of a new home. This includes agent's commission, legal and mortgage discharge costs on sale of existing home and the legal, stamp duty, valuation, and pest inspection costs on the purchase of the new home. These costs are capped at $_____ in total.

Payment of sale and purchase costs is dependent upon prior confirmation of both sale of existing home and purchase of new home taking place. Both sale and purchase must be completed within 12 months of transfer.

For those employees looking to buy a home in the new location, the company will pay the cost of accommodation up to a four-month period in a serviced apartment or leased home. Employees who have this facility are unable to apply for rental assistance.

3.2 Financial Assistance for those selling and buying a home in a higher cost city.

Special financial support will be made available to assist employees with the purchase of a new home when moving to a higher-cost city. This support is not available to those who wish to retain their current home and purchase a second new home nor is it available for investment purposes.

3.3 Employees who rent in current location and rent in new location.

The company will pay costs associated with having to terminate an existing lease. Employees who used to rent in old location and rent in new location will be paid rental assistance based on the difference between rent paid in old location and rent paid in new location. The reimbursement will be up to 100% of the net rental gap.

Relocating to a higher cost city.

Rental subsidy applies only to those relocating to a higher cost city. Accommodation must be comparable to that rented in old location. Recognising that distance from city centre and travel time are not comparable in different cities.

The company will offer a rental subsidy of 50% of the net difference between current rent and the rental paid in the new location, for an equivalent house or unit for a period of three years.

If the employee resides rent-free in current location, management discretion will apply taking these guidelines into account. The company will meet the cost of Fringe Benefits Tax where it is incurred.

Employees applying for the rental subsidy need to provide details indicating rental costs in their old location with a copy of the new lease agreement attached. Application is to be submitted to the Supervisor for approval and to arrange payment through payroll.

3.4 Employees who own their home and choose to rent it out and rent in new location.

Employees who rent out their home while they are in the new location are required to include amounts received as rent, by completing application for Rental Subsidy form, in determining assistance to be offered. The company will reimburse 100% of the net gap between net rental income received and rental paid in the new location for three years in a comparable property.

Any damage caused to the employee's property as a result of tenant exposure is the responsibility of the employee.

3.5 Employees who rent in current location and choose to buy in new higher cost location.

Employees who are renting and wish to buy are improving their situation and as such receive no assistance. At Supervisors discretion temporary accommodation may be provided while employee looks for new home (not to exceed 3 months and inclusive of Transfer accommodation referred to in this document).

3.6 Payment of Rental Bond.

Employees are responsible for paying the bond on any rented property.

3.7 Employees who own home and leave it vacant and rent in new location.

Where an employee transfers and keeps the accommodation in the old location vacant, rental assistance will be made available with Supervisor approval. Employees who transfer with their family for periods of more than 6 months are encouraged to rent their existing home in the old location.

3.7 Employees who transfer leaving partner and dependents in current location and rent in new location.

Employees transferring on a temporary basis without their partner/family will be provided with fully furnished accommodation, with laundry and kitchen facilities. All reasonable costs associated with the transfer for phone, electricity, and the company will pay gas. The cost of accommodation will be fully met by the company.

A settlement allowance of $_____ a week will be paid to the employee to cover costs associated with maintaining the two households. This allowance is grossed up and paid through payroll. The employee is expected to meet costs of food and laundry.

4. Levels of Relocation Services and Entitlements.

Recommend:

- that all services other than those that involve financial payments direct to the employee be managed by an outsourced vendor;
- this policy document become the basis for a Service Level Agreement with an outsource vendor; and
- once the decision to transfer has been made, the employee will manage all services through the outsource provider;
- the employee's Supervisor will select from a choice of three levels (the level of service the outsourced provider will provide);
- the employee will be given a pack reflecting all the services and entitlements they can expect;
- there should be some degree of flexibility in providing relocation services depending on the circumstances of the individual relocating. This flexibility will reside with the employee's Supervisor; and
- where there are large volumes of employees relocating, it may be necessary to appoint a dedicated or partly dedicated resource to coordinate the relocation and manage the administration side.

4.1 Return Flights.

Employees who do not relocate with their partner/immediate family will have made available to them two return flights per month. Employees may use these flights for themselves to return to their original location or may use the ticket for their partner to visit them in the new location. Flights will not be provided for the whole family.

Employees who relocate on a temporary basis with their partner/family will have made available to them two flights per year to return to the original location for themselves and their family. Wherever possible, discounted fares are to be used.

Return flights are to be planned in advance and are to be booked at least five days before departure to enable discount tickets to be used. Arrangements for these return trips are to be made via the new Supervisor.

4.2 Returning home after temporary transfer.

The company will pay costs associated with employee returning home after the temporary transfer, such as removal expenses of personal effects and car.

Chapter 13

Resignation

Termination Terms and Conditions.

If you decide to resign from (Company), you will need to provide two weeks' notice in writing to your Supervisor.

If (Company) terminates your employment, you are entitled to two weeks' notice if you have less than three years' service with (Company) three weeks' notice for three to five years' service, and four weeks' notice if you have five or more years' service. An additional one-week's notice shall be given if you are over 45 years of age and have had a minimum of two years' service with (Company). In the case of serious misconduct, your employment may be terminated immediately.

(Company) may, at its option, make a payment in lieu of any notice period to which you or (Company) is entitled. In the event of termination, you will be paid any accrued annual or long service leave entitlements, in addition to any notice or pay in lieu of notice.

(Company) will notify the Superannuation Plan of the termination of your employment and they will contact you about your superannuation benefits.

You will be required to return all (Company) property including items such as security passes, keys, computers etc. upon termination of your employment with (Company).

An employee who wishes to resign from his/her employment with (Company) should provide advance verbal and written notice in accordance with his/her individual Contract of Employment. This notice allows (Company) to prepare for a suitable replacement and to calculate the employee's final payment of salary, including overtime (if applicable), and accrued but unused, Annual Leave etc.

If the employee does not provide the required or agreed amount of notice, the Company may request the person to forfeit the equivalent salary.

In the majority of instances, the employee will be expected to continue to perform his/her duties up to the date of resignation. However, (Company) may request the termination of the employee's services at any time during the period of notice and will pay the appropriate amount of salary in lieu.

Certificate of Service

Confirms the length of employment, last position held and reason for leaving will be the only written reference provided by the Company which is provided on request.

Company Property

Must be returned to the Company prior to termination.

Exit Interviews

Refers to the process whereby employees are provided with an opportunity to provide feedback to the organisation prior to their leaving. A questionnaire may be sent to the person leaving or one-on-one meeting may be arranged with a Human Resources representative.

Reasons why an individual voluntarily leaves their position can be complex and diverse. Exit interviews are designed to obtain information from departing employees about why they chose to leave. Information from exit interviews will be used to create a work environment that encourages people to remain working with the company and to thrive in their working environment.

All employees who decide to leave (Company) will either:

- will complete an exit interview questionnaire within their last week or shortly after their termination of employment. Or

- have a face-to-face or telephone interview with a member of Human Resources Department.

Confidentiality:

All information obtained in these interviews will be held in the strictest confidence as is data obtained from a face-to- face interview and the completed exit interview form.

Final Pay

Refers to the payment of entitlements up to and including the date employment terminates and includes:

- salary due to the date of termination;
- overtime or accrued time (if applicable);
- accrued Annual Leave;
- accrued entitled Long Service Leave;
- less any reimbursements for training as per 'Employee Training agreement'

Giving notice

Refers to employees who voluntarily terminate their employment providing verbal and written notice of the date they will leave and the reason for leaving. The majority of employees are required to provide a minimum of two (2) weeks' notice. Actual required notice is documented in individual employment contracts.

Superannuation

Entitlements from (Superannuation Fund) may not be available on the last day of employment. The Staff Superannuation Fund will contact people after termination.

The Employee will:

- inform his/her Supervisor both verbally and in writing of the intention to resign.
- complete an 'Exit Interview Form'

- provide the minimum required notice as per their employment contract.
- return Company property to their Supervisor prior to leaving.
- continue to observe all requirements of their employment contract and (Company) policies during the notice period.

When a Supervisor receives advice from a contractor or temporary agency employee that they will be ceasing employment with (Company) or where the temporary employee's assignment has ended, the following procedures will be followed:

- Supervisor negotiates a final working day, giving due consideration to projects and workload for his/her Business Area;
- Supervisor ensures that on the external contractor's or temporary agency employee's final working day, that any (company) property they have provided during his/her employment (i.e.: security pass, laptop, procedures manuals etc.) are collected; and have checked 'Property Declaration' for details. The next business day after employee's final day of work, the Supervisor logs a call with (Company) Support Centre to cancel all IT user accounts for that employee.

Severance Pay

All employees are entitled to severance pay after one full calendar year's service. Severance pay is based on a sliding scale. If (Company) needs to instigate the termination of a full-time employee's service for reasons other than dismissal, the company endorses some payment based on legislation.

Entitlements are based on basic pay (i.e.: excluding overtime, allowances, penalties, and bonuses). For every year of service, the employee will receive one week of salary or wage.

Chapter 14

Training and Development

Training begins at the onset of an employee's employment with (Company). Often, the first sign is when there is a gap between the employee's abilities and the requirements of the position. The second sign that training is necessary is when problems occur either in the productivity and/or behaviour of employees. This policy establishes (Company's) responsibility to employees regarding training and development of all employees. The information contained in this document represents the way (Company) manages the training and development function. This document has been deemed to be a living document and will be varied when and where necessary.

(Company) is committed to developing the skills and knowledge of our people in order to grow the business. Higher levels of motivation, retention and job satisfaction are the key outcomes for employees who have access to timely, relevant and accessible training and development programs. The learning will be transferred to the business, resulting in increased levels of innovation, customer service and profitability. In addition, training and development becomes a crucial tool to manage organisational change and assist with the creation of a corporate identity. This policy applies to all (Company) personnel.

Training needs will be identified, and all training coordinated in a timely, professional manner. (Company's) primary training delivery strategy will be participative training that is practical vs. theoretical based. Employees will be involved in activities designed to share experiences and discover new information using a range of training methods designed to promote active participation and commitment to learning.

With the assistance of the Supervisors, (Company's) Training Department will determine specific training needs and whenever possible, prepare in-house training to meet those needs. If this is not possible or feasible, the training department will investigate to determine the best outsourcing to meet the training needs.

At the end of the each training course/workshop/seminar, the employee will be asked to evaluate the relevancy of the training as it relates to the training needs they were hoping to meet. Six weeks after the completion of training, the Supervisor and the trainee will evaluate how well the training met the training needs determined before the employee attended the training.

Where possible, (Company's) Training and Development will be the first providers of all training services within (Company). This will ensure that the culture, values and integrity of service excellence expected within (Company) will be maintained through the consistent application of training services across all business units.

Only where training cannot be delivered by Training and Development, or where it is not cost effective to deliver training internally, will (Company) resource and authorise the use of external providers. No external training provider is to be used without the prior authorisation of the Training and Development Manager.

Costs of Training

The cost of training is to be allocated to the appropriate cost centre of the employee. If the training is to enhance the skills and knowledge of employees, then this will be budgeted from the Human Resources (Training and Development) cost centre budget.

The Supervisor of the cost centre may authorise invoices under $_____ but invoices over $_____ need to be authorised by the Department Head.

Access to training

Training is highly regarded in (Company) and is offered to all employees equally. It serves several purposes and is achieved by ensuring that employees are exposed to training that will assist them in achieving their career and personal development plans. The Human Resources Department will co-ordinate all training programs.

Whenever possible, (Company) trainers who have the capability to conduct the required training will be used. If this is not possible, the Training Manager will source and select the training organisation that best meets the training need, determine training dates and venue. External Training will be assessed to determine the best available method of providing the training. The training organisation will provide all details and quotations in writing either via email or fax. Usually this will take the form of a training agreement that includes all costs and cancellation clauses.

Training needs will be identified via the following methods:

- performance appraisals;
- formal training needs analysis conducted twice a year;
- problems in production or work output;
- from 360o feedback;
- whenever company-wide changes require training to accommodate those changes;
- technical advances trigger a need for upgrading of a skill;
- morale problems;
- accident statistics;
- client complaints;
- union requirements;
- from the employees themselves;
- from Supervisors;
- from exit interviews with former employees that identify what training needs had not been met;

- from recruiters who can't supply the required skill mix; and
- where there is a gap between the qualifications of an employee and the needs of the position.

Performance Appraisals:

Performance Appraisals are conducted just before the new employee's probationary period is over and once a year thereafter. In the performance development section of the Performance Appraisal form, the employee can express his/her desire to receive training. In another section, the employee's Supervisor approves of or recommends other training for the employee. However, Supervisors are encouraged to stay alert for training requirements throughout the year and not rely specifically on performance appraisals to stimulate requests for required training.

360° Feedback

There are many ways that Supervisors can receive feedback from their staff. One popular method used extensively in business is a form of 360° Feedback. Not only do employees and their Supervisors evaluate their effectiveness, but peers and direct reports do as well.

360° feedback provides a number of benefits. It can:

- identify the importance of strong leadership, management and staff behaviours in business;
- build accountability for those behaviours;
- develop skills in providing constructive feedback and communication around business-related performance issues;
- identify development needs of employees so that they can further contribute to the business; and
- provide additional input to the Performance Appraisal process.

Training Requests

- All requests for training will be made by the Supervisor to the Training Department, who will then determine the best way to meet the training need. The training request may be received:
    - through a meeting or discussion;
    - a request sent via a Training Needs Analysis; or
    - requested in personal development section of the employee's Performance Appraisal form.

Twice a year, after training needs are analysed, the Training Department will schedule company-wide training. Information about scheduled training will be sent via email to all Supervisors to pass on to their employees who require training. Those who wish to attend training sessions must confirm two weeks before the training commences, especially in cases where outsourced trainers are used due to cancellation charges.

Responsibilities of Employees

- at commencement of employment with the company employee will sign 'Employee Training Agreement';
- complete the Professional Development area on their performance appraisal relating to training requirements;
- inform Supervisor when a training need is identified;
- register for relevant training;
- complete course work related to training and finishing the training;
- evaluate the training; and
- apply the new concepts and skills.

Traineeships

Traineeships occur where work is combined with structured training. It's important that the Traineeships are set up to meet the needs of both the employee and the company.

All Traineeships are to be managed to ensure that the participants' needs are achieved and that the courses run as smoothly and effectively as possible.

Study Assistance

(Company) encourages all individuals to undertake external training and development to assist them with their development and career progression. (Company) may provide financial assistance to individuals to undertake approved courses of study.

The objectives of this Study Assistance Policy are to clarify study provisions, to provide a consistent and fair approach to the provision of education assistance and to identify where accountabilities lie.

Eligibility

All permanent employees are eligible for Study Assistance provided the following criteria are met:

1. they have been employed for a minimum period of 12 months;
2. achievement of "Effective Performance" or higher in their last performance review;
3. proposed education program identified in Development Plan of Performance Appraisal to enhance performance in current job;
4. proposed education program congruent with the individual's long term career objectives; and
5. there is provision in the Training and Development budget.

Eligible Education Programs

To qualify for Study Assistance, the eligible education program must:

1. be relevant and appropriate to (Company's) business needs;
2. be provided by a recognised industry or education institution; and
3. provide a recognised qualification upon completion, i.e.: undergraduate or post-graduate qualification, ASFA qualification, etc.

Lectures/Tutorial Leave

- up to 4 hours of paid leave per week is available for attending lectures/tutorials, provided the lectures/tutorials are not available outside normal work hours; and
- any time off must be agreed to in advance with the Supervisor.

Study Leave

Study Leave is defined as time away from work for the purposes of preparing for and attending exams, completing major assignments or specific course work. Supervisors are expected to be supportive of individuals who are studying. Study leave can be:

- up to 1.5 days per subject/unit per semester (a total of six days per year);
- increased use of flexible working hours or other leave;
- granted on condition that the individual continues to complete his/her normal work duties and is not cumulative;
- varied by Supervisors at their discretion based on work commitments and business needs; and
- taken only when appropriate notice has been given to the Supervisor.

Fee Structure

The following fees will be reimbursed upon the successful completion (i.e.: passing) of the semester or year:

For Undergraduate or Industry Programs

- 100% of up-front fees, and administration fees will be subject to reimbursement;
- fees for that portion of the course that was undertaken while working at (Company); and
- fees will be debited from the Training and Development cost centre upon the employee's Supervisor's approval and approval from the Training and Development Manager.

For Post-Graduate Programs excluding Masters Programs i.e. MBA

- 75% of up-front fees and administration fees will be reimbursed each semester. If fees are deferred under HECS, only the up-front amount will be subject to reimbursement;
- fees will be debited from the Training and Development Cost Centre upon the approval of the Supervisor and the Training and Development Manager; and
- a total limit of $____ will apply to reimbursement of Post-Graduate Programs.

For Masters Programs i.e.: MBA

- 50% of up-front fees and administration fees will be reimbursed each semester;
- fees will be debited from the Training and Development Cost Centre upon the approval of the Supervisor and the Training and Development Manager; and
- a total limit of $____will apply to reimbursement of Masters' Programs.

Textbooks and Incidentals

- Money spent on textbooks and incidental expenses will not be reimbursed.

Resignation of Employment

Individuals who resign from (Company) will not be eligible for reimbursement.

Failing a Subject

If the individual fails a subject, there is no guarantee that approval will be granted for further Study Assistance.

Reimbursement of Fees

The individual will:

1. if employee requires payment before taking course, 'Study Fees Advance Payment' Form;
2. if employee does not require up-front payment, complete a 'Study Assistance Reimbursement' Form attaching a photocopy of confirmation from the education institution of exam results and receipts for any fees paid. For monies to be paid directly into the bank account, complete a Direct Credit Reimbursement form, obtained from Accounts Payable; and
3. forward forms and attachments to his/her Supervisor.

Employment Training Agreement

New employees will sign an agreement that if they leave the company within two (2) years of obtaining specialised company-paid training that they will reimburse (Company) for the training on a pro-rated basis. For instance, if staff member leaves (Company) six (6) months after receiving training, s/he would refund (Company) 75% of the cost of training expenses. These funds would be deducted from staff member's final employment payment.

Chapter 15

Work Cover

Workers Compensation

All employees of (Company) are covered under the Workers' Compensation Act while at work. These laws vary from State to State and from position to position. The workers' compensation laws exist to ensure employees are properly protected in the event of an accident or injury while they're at work.

All accidents or injuries sustained in the work environment are to be reported immediately. Failure to do so may result in a non-payment of insurance. It is the policy of (Company) that all accidents or injuries are reported regardless of the severity. It is the employee's responsibility to inform the Supervisor of accidents or injuries at the time of the incident. An accident logbook is located at the first aid station.

Rehabilitation Policy

(Company) realises that there are substantial benefits for employees and employers resulting from an employee's early return to work after an injury. Experience shows that work assists the healing process and helps restore the worker's normal functions sooner.

Workplace Rehabilitation is a managed process involving early provision of necessary and reasonable services. This includes suitable duties programs when practicable, to ensure the worker's earliest possible return to work or if return to work is precluded, to maximise the worker's independent functioning.

(Company) has a commitment to preventing injury and illness through providing a safe and healthy working environment. The objectives of this Rehabilitation Program are as follows:

- Rehabilitation is normal practice and an expectation within this workplace.
- Rehabilitation commences as soon as practicable after the injury, with approval of the worker's treating doctor.
- The goal, through a rehabilitation plan, is to return the injured person to their normal duties.
- A team approach to rehabilitation is used, with cooperation, consultation and confidentiality being key requirements for all persons involved.
- At all times the rights, welfare and confidentiality of the worker are respected.
- This Rehabilitation Policy and Procedures and overall result of our program are regularly reviewed and continuously improved. The date of the next review is _____.
- A trained Rehabilitation Coordinator has been appointed in the Human Resources area to effectively manage our Rehabilitation program. Where appropriate, external rehabilitation providers will be engaged to provide additional expertise.
- No worker is disadvantaged by participation in a Workplace Rehabilitation program.

This Rehabilitation Policy will ensure the joint cooperation of management and workers.

The term 'worker' is used to represent all employees of the Company.

Conclusion

Keep in mind that your company Employee Handbook should cover all the rules and regulations that an employee is expected to know and follow. They are an employee's guide that explains a company's rules and regulations.

On the first day of the person's employment, s/he is given a copy of the company Employee Handbook and after a week is asked to sign an agreement stating that s/he has read the handbook and understands its content. This way both employees and employers are protected.

- The employee will be protected because s/he will know the company rules and regulations.

- The employer will be protected because if the employee broke any of the company rules and regulations s/he won't be able to claim innocence if s/he has confirmed that s/he knew and understood them.

www.ingramcontent.com/pod-product-compliance
Lightning Source LLC
Chambersburg PA
CBHW050512210326
41521CB00011B/2430